T0063679

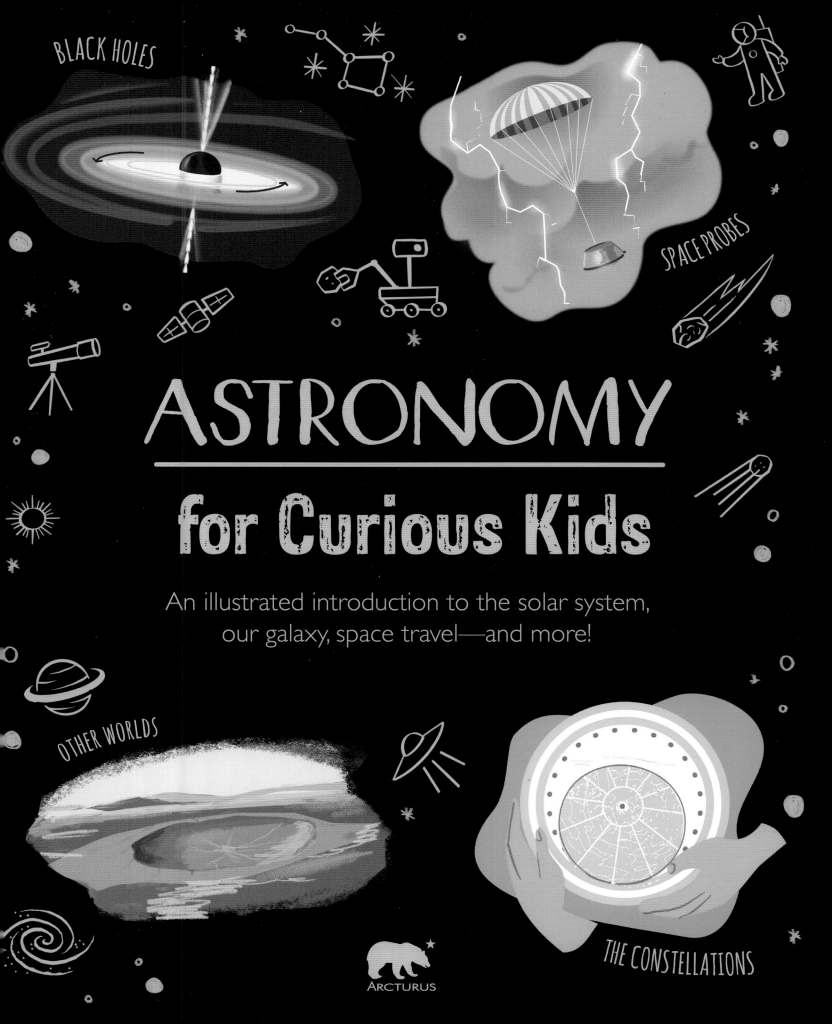

BLACK HOLES

SPACE PROBES

ASTRONOMY
for Curious Kids

An illustrated introduction to the solar system,
our galaxy, space travel—and more!

OTHER WORLDS

THE CONSTELLATIONS

ARCTURUS

ARCTURUS

This edition published in 2023 by Arcturus Publishing Limited
26/27 Bickels Yard, 151–153 Bermondsey Street,
London SE1 3HA

Copyright © Arcturus Holdings Limited

All rights reserved. No part of this publication may be reproduced,
stored in a retrieval system, or transmitted, in any form or by any means,
electronic, mechanical, photocopying, recording, or otherwise, without
prior written permission in accordance with the provisions of the
Copyright Act 1956 (as amended). Any person or persons who do any
unauthorized act in relation to this publication may be liable to criminal
prosecution and civil claims for damages.

Author: Giles Sparrow
Illustrator: Nik Neves
Consultant: Helen Giles
Designer: Dani Leigh
Editors: Lydia Halliday, William Potter

ISBN: 978-1-3988-3097-4
CH010948US
Supplier 29, Date 0523, PI 00003556

Printed in China

CONTENTS

WELCOME TO ASTRONOMY

If you've ever looked up at the night sky and wondered just what all those different stars and other lights are, you've already taken your first step into the amazing world of astronomy. People have asked the same questions for thousands of years, and astronomers are the people who try to answer them. These include some of the biggest questions you can think of, such as:

Where did everything come from?
Is there life on other planets?
How do stars shine?
How big is the Universe?
Will the Universe ever come to an end?

This book may not be able to answer all of these questions, because often the answers are still unknown. However, it will explain the latest theories about these and many other aspects of the Universe, and show you how astronomers use ingenious tools and clever thinking to better understand objects separated from Earth by the vast reaches of outer space.

◉ GOLDEN RULES

To get the most out of an evening's stargazing, here are a few things to keep in mind …

Wait for the darkness

After the Sun sets, the sky will be light for a fairly long period known as twilight. The farther the Sun is below the horizon, the darker the sky will be, and the stars will stand out better against it. Serious stargazers may wait for up to two hours for the sky to become fully dark.

Avoid light pollution

Light shining up from streetlights can make the sky itself glow, drowning out all but the brightest stars—a problem that's called light pollution. To see the night sky properly, try to get far away from city lights, but always stay safe and make sure people know where you are—stargazing is more fun shared with a group!

Beware of the ripples

When days are warm but nights are cold, warm air rising off the land can cause apparently clear skies to ripple. This deflects the paths of light rays, so that bright stars twinkle and faint ones may be even fainter. Windy weather can have the same effect.

◉ YOUR AMAZING EYES

Your eyes are natural cameras. Light enters through the black central pupil and is detected by light-sensitive cells at the back of the eye, or retina. The pupil usually stays small to control the light getting in, but it gets wider in the dark, while the retina cells become more sensitive. An average person's eyesight will let them see around 3,000 stars on a clear night, and the farthest thing most people can see is the Andromeda Galaxy, 2.5 million light years away.

◉ NIGHT VISION

It can take an hour or more for your eyes to adjust properly to darkness and just a moment to undo that good work. For this reason, even if you can't avoid light pollution in the sky, try to find an observing spot that protects you from the direct glare of streetlights, car headlights, and other bright lights.

Everything in the night sky seems to be on the move. Some of these movements are real, and some are due to the fact that Earth itself is spinning and moving through space. It's important to understand the difference.

⭐ THE CHANGING SKY

Even watching the stars for a few minutes will show you the most obvious and regular change in the sky. Each night, stars rise from the east and set in the west, or spin in slow circles around a point in the sky. Long-exposure photographs can capture this movement in beautiful star trails.

⭐ STAR MOVEMENTS

The stars that are on view change through the night because Earth is a huge ball spinning in space. At any moment, half the sky lies below the horizon, but as Earth's spin changes your point of view, new stars come into view from the east, while others sink below the western horizon.

The Sun's glare drowns out the light of the stars closest to it, but that, too, changes. Earth is orbiting the Sun, and so the Sun's direction shifts from day to day, moving against the background stars, so that different ones are hidden by the glare at different times of year.

Aside from effects linked to Earth's spin and orbit, the stars move only very slowly. They are so far away that their actual movement through space appears tiny, and star patterns stay the same for thousands of years.

⭐ SOLAR SYSTEM WANDERERS

The Moon, planets, and other objects that lie within our own solar system behave differently from the spinning stars outside it. These objects are close enough for us to see their movements as they orbit the Sun at different speeds and appear against different background stars. What's more, this motion is complicated by the fact that our viewpoint on Earth is also circling the Sun once every year.

⭐ BASIC EQUIPMENT

If you want to track sky changes from night to night and season to season, spot the wandering planets, and learn the patterns of the stars, some basic equipment will help you get more out of your stargazing.

A magnetic compass (or smartphone compass app) will help you learn the different directions from your observing spot and quickly get your bearings. Use a notepad and pencil to record what you see. Sketch the patterns of the bright stars that are overhead when it's completely dark and then again an hour later to see how they've changed. A flashlight with red plastic taped over the beam will help you see your way in the dark without ruining your night vision.

⭐ FINDING YOUR WAY

If you have a smartphone, there are plenty of apps that show what you can see in the night sky, but a simple device called a planisphere (also known as a star wheel) may give you a better understanding of what's going on. The planisphere has two disks— when you rotate the upper one so that the time of day around the edge matches the correct date on the lower disk, the clear window shows you a map of which stars are currently over the horizon.

PLANISPHERE

BINOCULARS AND TELESCOPES

Your eyes can see a lot on their own, but you'll see even more of the Universe with binoculars or a telescope. Both of these optical instruments capture more light and create magnified views of the sky that reveal more detail.

BINOCULAR STARGAZING

Binoculars are great for sweeping large areas of sky. Their big lenses direct more light to your eyes, making stars appear brighter, and they reveal objects that are too faint to spot with your eyes alone. Most binoculars don't magnify much, though—this means that things look only a few times bigger. However, they are easy to point and hold steady.

TELESCOPIC ASTRONOMY

A small telescope may capture only a little more light than binoculars, but because it magnifies the view much more, it will make things appear much bigger and reveal greater detail in objects such as planets. Telescopes also magnify small motions (including your hands shaking), so they're usually mounted on a tripod.

TELESCOPE TYPES

Telescopes come in two main types. **Refractors** have a big lens at the front that collects light rays from distant stars and refracts (bends) them toward a focus point where they cross. **Reflectors** use two or more mirrors that bounce light rays onto paths that cross at the focus. Both types of telescopes feature another lens called an eyepiece to create a magnified image.

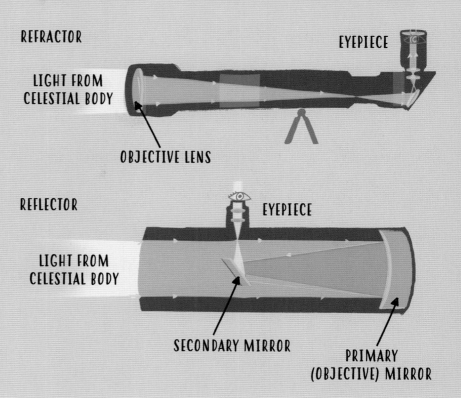

REFRACTOR

EYEPIECE

LIGHT FROM CELESTIAL BODY

OBJECTIVE LENS

REFLECTOR

EYEPIECE

LIGHT FROM CELESTIAL BODY

SECONDARY MIRROR

PRIMARY (OBJECTIVE) MIRROR

TELESCOPE MOUNTS

A mount holds the telescope in place while allowing it to swivel in different directions. In an **altazimuth** mount, a telescope can swing from side to side (parallel to the horizon) or up and down. An **equatorial** mount lines up with the celestial equator (see page 16). Then, the telescope can be pointed to objects using their celestial coordinates of **right ascension** and **declination**, like longtitude and latitude coordinates used on Earth's surface.

OUT OF CURIOSITY

Because light rays in a telescope cross over at the focus point, the image you see in the eyepiece is flipped left to right and upside down.

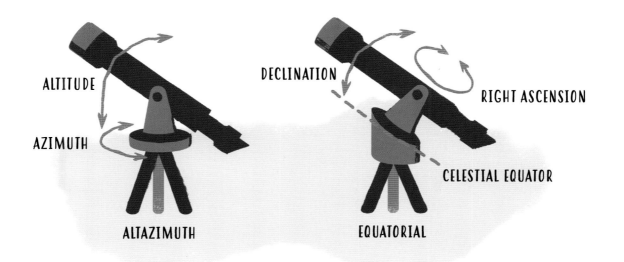

ALTITUDE

AZIMUTH

ALTAZIMUTH

DECLINATION

RIGHT ASCENSION

CELESTIAL EQUATOR

EQUATORIAL

CONSTELLATIONS

How can you make sense of all the lights in the night sky? Over many centuries, people have made patterns from the bright stars called constellations. These are a useful way of finding your way around the sky.

THE FIRST CONSTELLATIONS

Most constellations started out as groups of stars that people connected with imaginary lines to make pictures in the sky. Some look very much like the figure or object they're supposed to represent, while others take a lot of imagination! Taurus the bull is one of the most obvious patterns in the sky and dates back to at least 15,000 BCE—it's even found in cave paintings!

TWO STARS CALLED BETA AND ZETA TAURI FORM THE TIPS OF THE HORNS.

THE V-SHAPED HYADES STAR CLUSTER FORMS THE BULL'S FACE.

ALDEBARAN IS A GIANT RED STAR MARKING TAURUS' EYE.

WHAT MAKES A CONSTELLATION?

Constellations started out as figures drawn by linking stars in the sky, but once telescopes were invented, astronomers began to question which constellation each newly discovered star or other object should belong to. For this reason, today's constellations are defined as areas of the sky that fit together like a jigsaw puzzle, so it's clear where any newfound object belongs.

♌ CHANGING DEFINITIONS

Most constellations are made of stars that lie in the same direction as seen from Earth—they're not necessarily close together in space. For example, the brightest objects in Orion the Hunter are separated by vast distances.

- Rigel—knee—860 light years away
- Belelgeuse—right shoulder—548 light years away
- Bellatrix—left shoulder—200 light years away
- Orion's belt (Mintaka, Alnilam, Alnitak)—1,200, 2,000, and 1,260 light years away
- Orion Nebula—sword—1,400 light years away

♌ NAMING STARS

Many stars have names that were invented by Islamic astronomers more than a thousand years ago, but rather than memorizing these, you can use an easier system that uses the letters of the Greek alphabet. Each bright star in a constellation has a Greek letter applied to it that indicates its rank in the constellation, beginning with alpha and ending at omega for the twenty-fourth brightest star (since there are 24 letters in the Greek alphabet). This is written with a special form of the constellation name to indicate that it belongs in that particular star pattern. So, for example, Alpha Centauri is the brightest star in Centaurus, while Zeta Tauri is the sixth-brightest star in Taurus.

♌ THE MODERN CONSTELLATIONS

Today, there are 88 official constellations. Of these, 48 are ancient European and Middle Eastern star patterns that were listed by the Greek–Egyptian astronomer Ptolemy around 150 CE. The others were invented by various astronomers from the late 1400s to the 1700s, either to fill gaps between Ptolemy's constellations or to divide up parts of the far southern sky that ancient Eurasian astronomers never saw.

1	α	Alpha
2	β	Beta
3	γ	Gamma
4	δ	Delta
5	ε	Epsilon
6	ζ	Zeta
7	η	Eta
8	θ	Theta
9	ι	Iota
10	κ	Kappa
11	λ	Lambda
12	μ	Mu
13	ν	Nu
14	ξ	Xi
15	o	Omicron
16	π	Pi
17	ρ	Rho
18	σ	Sigma
19	τ	Tau
20	υ	Upsilon
21	φ	Phi
22	χ	Chi
23	ψ	Psi
24	ω	Omega

THE MEASURE OF THE SKY

Even though the distance to stars varies hugely, astronomers often treat them as lying on the surface of a huge sphere surrounding Earth. This imaginary shell called the celestial sphere helps astronomers record the directions of objects in the sky and the angles between them.

THE CELESTIAL SPHERE

To help explain the relationship between Earth and the sky, the celestial sphere copies many of Earth's own features. It spins around two fixed points called the north and south celestial poles (NCP and SCP), which lie directly above Earth's own north and south poles. It rotates from east to west once each day (reflecting what is really Earth's own west-to-east rotation), and a celestial equator midway between the two poles divides it into northern and southern hemispheres, just like Earth.

POSITIONS ON THE CELESTIAL SPHERE

Astronomers usually measure the locations of objects on the celestial sphere with a system that's similar to the longitude and latitude used on Earth. Objects have a declination between 0 and 90 degrees, which indicates how far north or south of the celestial equator they lie (+90° is the NCP, -90° is the SCP). They also have a right ascension, which indicates how far east or west they are from a fixed point called the First Point of Aries. This is measured in hours, minutes, and seconds rather than degrees. It indicates how far the object lags behind the First Point in its daily rotation around the sky.

WHAT CAN YOU SEE?

At any location on Earth, you can always see the celestial pole that matches your own hemisphere, lying in the direction of the nearest pole of Earth itself. This means that stargazers in the northern hemisphere see the NCP due north, and those in the southern hemisphere see the SCP due south.

The height of the pole above the horizon depends on your latitude. At Earth's own poles the celestial poles are directly overhead at the **zenith** point, but they sink steadily farther toward the horizon as you get closer to the equator. The sky spins around the celestial pole you can see, with stars rising from the east and sinking to the west. Stars close enough to the celestial pole never actually disappear but make circles in the sky and are called circumpolar.

In the course of a year, all the stars in your own celestial hemisphere will eventually come into view. However, the closer you get to the equator, the higher the line of the celestial equator rises up in the sky in the opposite direction to the celestial pole. Beneath it, you can see stars that lie in the opposite celestial hemisphere.

Stars that set completely are at their highest in the sky when they cross a line called the **meridian**, which runs north to south across the sky through the zenith.

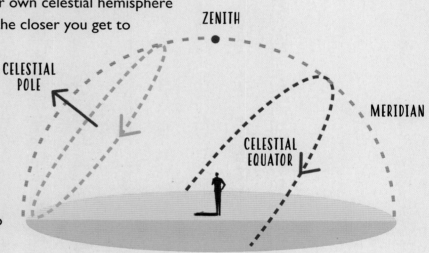

ANGLES IN THE SKY

Angles in the sky are generally measured in degrees. There are 360 degrees in a full circle and 90 degrees in a quarter circle (for instance, from the horizon to the zenith). The full moon is about half a degree across. Held at arm's length, your hand can provide a handy guide for estimating the size of different angles.

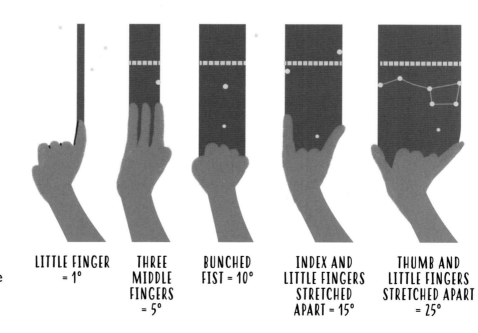

LITTLE FINGER = 1°

THREE MIDDLE FINGERS = 5°

BUNCHED FIST = 10°

INDEX AND LITTLE FINGERS STRETCHED APART = 15°

THUMB AND LITTLE FINGERS STRETCHED APART = 25°

STAR-HOPPING

The quickest way to find your way around the sky is to use a trick called star-hopping, where you follow imaginary lines between stars to find your way to other stars and interesting points in the sky.

THE FAR NORTH

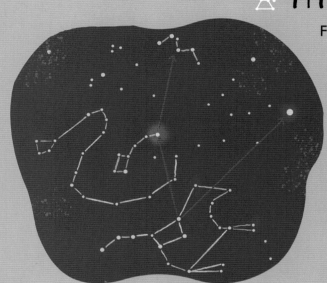

For northern-hemisphere stargazers, the sky seems to rotate around the pole star Polaris, the brightest star in Ursa Minor, the Little Bear (or Little Dipper). To find it, follow a line from the two "pointer" stars on the end of the Big Dipper or Plough (a pattern made by the seven brightest stars in Ursa Major, the Great Bear).

Continue past Polaris to find the bright W-shape of Cassiopeia, and follow a line across the top of the Big Dipper to find the bright-yellow star Capella (in Auriga, the Charioteer).

A MILKY WAY TRIANGLE

Around August and September, three bright stars mark out a large triangle in the southern sky for stargazers in the northern hemisphere. Deneb is the brightest star in Cygnus the Swan, Vega is the brightest in Lyra the Lyre, and Altair is the brightest in Aquila the Eagle. The same pattern appears upside down in the north for southern-hemisphere skywatchers.

Scan the middle of the triangle with binoculars to see pale clouds of distant stars, compact star clusters and other beautiful sights in the Milky Way, then follow the outstretched neck of Cygnus south to reach Scorpius the Scorpion, Sagittarius the Archer, and the center of our galaxy.

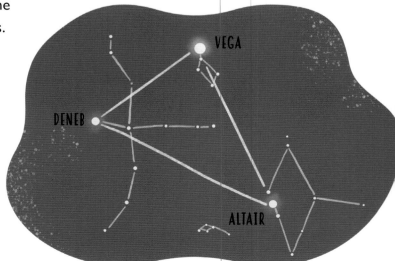

ORION AND NEARBY STARS

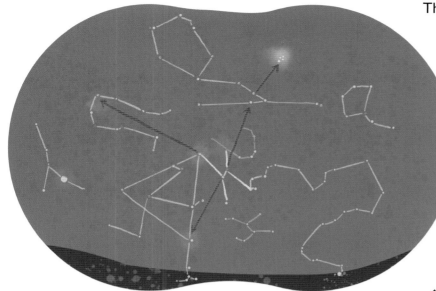

The distinctive constellation of Orion the Hunter lies near the celestial equator and is at its best in both hemispheres on evenings from December through to March. Northern hemisphere observers can see it over the southern horizon, while southern stargazers should look for it upside down in the northern sky.

Various stars in Orion point to other interesting objects. A line southeast from its belt points to Sirius, the brightest star in the sky, in the constellation of Canis Major, the Great Dog. A line northeast from the belt leads to Aldebaran (the eye of Taurus the Bull) and beyond it to the beautiful Pleiades star cluster. A line from the middle of the belt past brilliant-red Betelgeuse on Orion's shoulder leads to Castor and Pollux, the bright twin stars that give the constellation Gemini its name. You can also imagine an equilateral triangle connecting Sirius, Betelgeuse, and Procyon—the brightest star of Canis Minor, the Lesser Dog.

THE SOUTHERN CROSS AND BEYOND

Unlike Polaris at the North Celestial Pole, there's no bright star to mark the South Celestial Pole (SCP). Southern-hemisphere stargazers can best locate it using the the small but brilliant constellation of Crux, the Southern Cross.

Look east along the shorter bar of Crux to find another pair of bright stars, Beta and Alpha Centauri, then imagine that they form the short bar of a similar cross. Follow imaginary lines down the long bars of these two crosses, and they'll meet very close to the SCP, with the faint star Sigma Octantis lying nearby. Extend the lines past the pole to find the Small and Large Magellanic Clouds, two satellite galaxies of our Milky Way.

SEASONS AND THE ZODIAC

Every year, as Earth makes its orbit around the Sun, the Sun appears to pass through a band of constellations called the zodiac. Because the planets move in roughly the same flat plane, this zodiac area isn't only where we find the Sun, but is where the planets live too.

SEASONAL CHANGES

Earth's seasons and the changing amount of daylight that each hemisphere experiences through the year arise because our planet's poles are tilted at an angle. North and south poles keep pointing in the same direction in space, but as Earth moves through its orbit, first one, then the other is angled more toward the Sun.

THE PLANE OF EARTH'S ORBIT IS CALLED THE ECLIPTIC.

NORTHERN AUTUMN EQUINOX, SEPTEMBER—BOTH HALVES OF EARTH GET EQUAL SUNLIGHT.

NORTHERN SUMMER SOLSTICE, JUNE—NORTH POLE IS ANGLED TOWARD THE SUN.

NORTHERN WINTER SOLSTICE, DECEMBER—SOUTH POLE IS ANGLED TOWARD THE SUN.

NORTHERN SPRING EQUINOX, MARCH—BOTH HALVES OF EARTH GET EQUAL SUNLIGHT.

EARTH'S POLES ARE TILTED AT 23.5° FROM UPRIGHT, SO THE ECLIPTIC IS TILTED AT 23.5° FROM THE CELESTIAL EQUATOR.

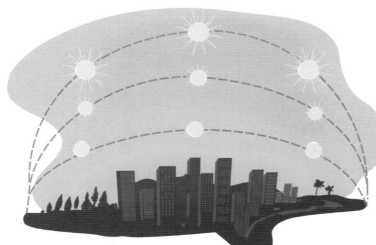

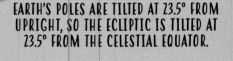 CHANGING DAYS

As each pole takes turns pointing toward the Sun, the Sun's daily path across the sky rises higher or sinks lower. In summer, the Sun rises higher in the sky, and days are longer than nights. In winter, the Sun skims low over the horizon, and days are shorter.

JOURNEY THROUGH THE ZODIAC

The Sun's apparent motion in the course of a year takes it along a line called the **ecliptic**. In this journey, the Sun moves through 12 major constellations, the signs of the zodiac. These are some of the oldest and most famous star patterns in the sky, with all but one representing animals or humans from ancient legends:

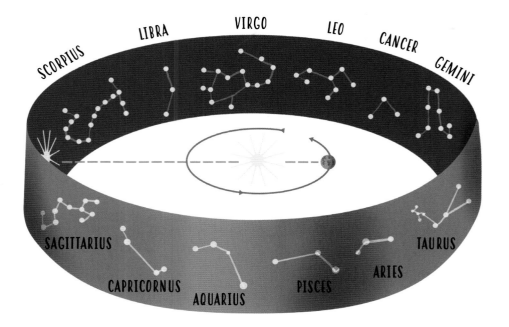

Aries	♈	the Ram
Taurus	♉	the Bull
Gemini	♊	the Twins
Cancer	♋	the Crab
Leo	♌	the Lion
Virgo	♍	the Maiden
Libra	♎	the Scales
Scorpius	♏	the Scorpion
Sagittarius	♐	the Archer
Capricornus	♑	the Sea Goat
Aquarius	♒	the Water Carrier
Pisces	♓	the Fish

The planets in our solar system follow their own paths around the sky but are only slightly tilted to the Sun's own path. This means that they can usually be found in one of the zodiac constellations.

OUT OF CURIOSITY

Astrology is the belief that the movement of the Sun and planets through the zodiac predicts or influences events on Earth. It's an ancient idea that inspired many early astronomers to try and understand the Universe. Even though we now know it's scientifically impossible, many people remain fascinated by the idea.

The 12 zodiac constellations are very different in size and shape, so the Sun spends different amounts of time in each. Astrologers divide the sky into 12 regular divisions called houses and say that each represents one zodiac constellation, even though the Sun may be in one house and a different constellation at the same time!

THIRTEENTH SIGN

Thanks to slow changes in Earth's orbit, the ecliptic path of the Sun today crosses a thirteenth constellation as well as the 12 ancient zodiac patterns. This thirteenth zodiac constellation is Ophiuchus, the Serpent Carrier, which the Sun passes between Scorpius and Sagittarius.

TOP TEN SIGHTS

Space is full of wonders, but you can get started on your skywatching journey by looking for these ten amazing sights.

The Moon

Earth's satellite changes appearance from night to night depending on the amount of sunlight shining on its Earth-facing side. See how many of its dark seas you can spot without help, then use binoculars for a closer look at its cratered surface.

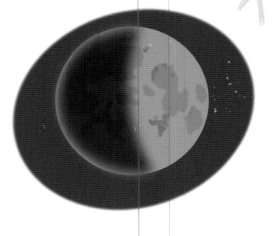

Lunar eclipse

On rare occasions, the Earth, Sun, and Moon are in alignment, and the Earth casts its shadow on the full moon. If the lineup is perfect, the Moon can appear reddish in color.

Moons of Jupiter

Binoculars will turn Jupiter, the largest planet in the solar system, into a small but brilliant circle. Four fainter lights dance around it from side to side. These are the planet's largest moons: Io, Europa, Ganymede, and Callisto.

Rings of Saturn

Look at Saturn, the most distant naked-eye planet, through binoculars, and you may see that it's not quite a perfect circle. A small telescope will show the planet's famous rings, a disk made up of countless icy fragments.

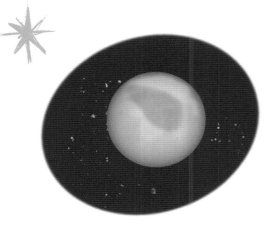

Mars

The red planet Mars changes a lot in both brightness and distance from Earth. When it's at its closest (called opposition), a small telescope can help you spot dark markings and maybe the bright gleam of its icy polar caps.

Albireo

Lots of stars come in pairs called binaries, but one of the prettiest of all is Albireo, which marks the beak of Cygnus the Swan. Look through binoculars or a telescope to see its bright-yellow and blue components.

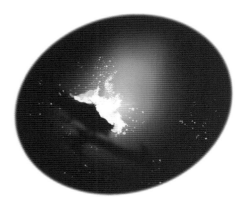

Orion Nebula

Stars are born in huge collapsing clouds of gas and dust, which light up from inside, causing them to glow. The Orion Nebula is the biggest and brightest of those visible from Earth, with a quartet of newborn stars in its heart.

Pleiades star cluster

This bright, compact group of stars in the constellation of Taurus the Bull contains at least a thousand stars, but is dominated by its brightest blue-white members. The Pleiades were seven sisters in Greek mythology, but most stargazers can only see six stars with the unaided eye. How many can you spot?

Andromeda Galaxy

Easily spotted with the naked eye under dark skies, a patch of light in the constellation of Andromeda is the star-packed core of the nearest large spiral galaxy to our own Milky Way. Binoculars or a small telescope will help you make out the pale disk around the central core.

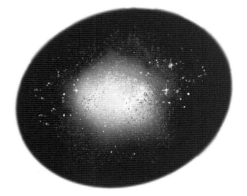

Messier 13 star cluster

This globular (ball-shaped) star cluster in the constellation of Hercules contains several hundred thousand old red and yellow stars so closely packed that they sometimes collide.

THE CUTTING EDGE

Professional astronomers don't spend much time staring through a telescope. Instead, they use computers to operate instruments at mountaintop observatories or collect data from telescopes in Earth's orbit and beyond.

ABOVE THE CLOUDS

Professional observatories are often sited on mountainous islands such as Hawaii and the Canary Islands, and on high, dry plains such as Chile's Atacama Desert. This puts them above most of Earth's atmosphere and clouds, improving the chances of crystal clear skies.

GIANT TELESCOPES

The world's biggest telescopes use mirrors to collect light. The Extremely Large Telescope currently being built in Chile, has a main mirror with 798 hexagonal segments that fit together to make a 39.3-m (130-ft) curved reflector. The largest single-mirror telescopes in the world are 8.4 m (27.6 ft) across.

TELESCOPES IN SPACE

Remote-controlled telescopes in space get a sharp view of the Universe with no distortion from Earth's atmosphere. They also benefit from permanent darkness, which allows them to observe for 24 hours a day. What's more, because Earth's atmosphere blocks many types of energy from space, some satellite telescopes can be used to study the Universe in entirely different ways.

The Hubble Space Telescope has delivered spectacular views of space in visible light for more than 30 years.

The James Webb Space Telescope's 6.5-m (21.4-ft) mirror picks up faint **infrared** or heat radiation from some of the coolest and most distant objects in the Universe.

The Chandra X-ray Observatory uses metal tubes to capture high-energy rays from some of the hottest stars and most violent cosmic events.

The Gaia satellite tracks tiny movements of stars, and maps our galaxy, the Milky Way.

OUT OF CURIOSITY

The world's biggest refractor telescope, at Yerkes Observatory in the USA, has a 1.02-m (40-in) lens. Lenses any larger than this are too heavy to move and absorb too much light to be useful.

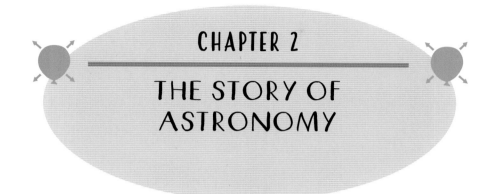

CHAPTER 2

THE STORY OF ASTRONOMY

People have been looking at the sky for thousands of years, and coming up with ways to explain and predict the movement of the stars and planets. As the tools we use to study the Universe have improved, so has our picture of how it really works.

In this chapter, we'll look at how astronomy has changed over the centuries and how astronomers, with new inventions, have changed our understanding of Earth's position in the cosmos.

The first people who looked at the night sky didn't keep a written record of their ideas about the Universe, but we can still figure out what they were studying from the traces they did leave behind.

π. STONE STARGAZERS

The prehistoric stone circle of Stonehenge in southern England was built around 5,000 years ago. Key stones point in the direction of sunrise at midsummer (the longest day), while a ring of pits could have been used to track the motion of the Moon, and perhaps predict when the Sun and Moon were likely to line up and cause an **eclipse**.

Every year, the rising and setting positions of the Sun move north or southward along the horizon, changing direction on the solstices (longest and shortest days). At Chankillo, in Peru, a series of towers built along a ridge mark the different points in this yearly journey, allowing skywatchers to use them as a calendar.

ⅠⅠ. MOON MAPPING

Most of the time, the Moon is the only object with details that can be seen from Earth with the unaided eye. The earliest known Moon maps were carved on rocks at a tomb in Knowth, Ireland, about 4,800 years ago.

Around the world, different peoples have seen patterns on the Moon's surface and told stories about them. In Europe and America, the most common of these is the "Man in the Moon." The dark areas of the Moon's surface can resemble that of a human face (see below). In China, people see either a princess or a "Moon Rabbit."

ⅠⅠ. THE SHIFTING STARS

As well as tracking the Sun, ancient people used the rising and setting of prominent stars through the year to keep track of time. In ancient Egypt, the rising of the brightest star, Sirius, just before sunrise in late July, was used to predict the annual flood season of the Nile River.

The Egyptians depicted Sirius as the goddess Sopdet, with a brilliant star on her head.

ANCIENT ASTRONOMY

Around 2,000 years ago in ancient Greece, astronomers came up with a theory to explain and predict how the stars and planets behave. This would hold sway for more than 1,500 years.

THE EARTH-CENTERED UNIVERSE

For ancient Greek astronomers, Earth was the biggest thing they could imagine, and they had no way of knowing the size or distance of objects in the sky. It made sense to believe that Earth was the center of the Universe, with the Moon, Sun, planets, and stars circling around it at various distances.

The Greeks imagined that celestial objects sat on transparent crystal spheres that circled around Earth at different rates.

OUT OF CURIOSITY

Not everyone thought that the Earth was the center of the Universe—a Greek astronomer named Aristarchus used clever observations to prove that the Sun was much larger than Earth. This was one of several reasons why he decided to place the Sun at the center of everything.

PROVING EARTH IS ROUND

Ancient Greek thinkers knew very well that Earth was a sphere, not a flat surface. Around 240 BCE, an astronomer named Eratosthenes even calculated the size of the Earth by showing how the Sun cast shadows of different lengths at different locations.

A clue to Earth's curved surface is that the masts and sails of ships sailing toward the horizon can be seen long after their hulls have disappeared from view.

PTOLEMY'S EPICYCLES

If the planets are circling around Earth, then why do they sometimes make backward loops in the sky? This was one of the biggest challenges to the Earth-centered theory of the Universe. However, in the second century CE, Egyptian astronomer Ptolemy came up with a clever solution called **epicycles**.

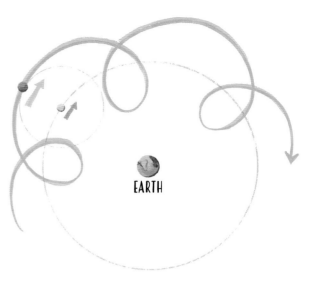

EARTH

An epicycle is a smaller circle centered on a larger one. Ptolemy suggested that the planets moved around epicycles, which circled around Earth on a larger orbit. Because of this, movement around the epicycle could sometimes slow down or even reverse a planet's general drift around the sky.

Ptolemy's idea of an Earth-centered Universe reamined the dominant theory for more than a thousand years, but many new ways of understanding and interpreting the stars were developing around the world. These led people to challenge the old theories.

ISLAM AND ASTRONOMY

Followers of the new religion of Islam, founded in the seventh century, had many reasons to be interested in the night sky. They began each month with the first sighting of a crescent moon after sunset. They also used the stars to decide the right times for prayers, and to discover the precise direction of the holy city of Mecca for praying and building mosques.

ASTROLABES AND ACCURACY

Astronomers in the Islamic world developed new tools for accurately measuring the position of objects in the sky, such as the **astrolabe**. Precise measurements showed that objects didn't always follow Ptolemy's theory, so clever thinkers such as Ibn al-Haytham (who lived in Iraq around the year 1000 CE) tweaked his ideas to make them fit.

An astrolabe is a metal circle with a loop at the top, so it can hang straight down. Marks around the edge divide the circle into 360 degrees, and a sighting bar pivots in the middle. By tilting the bar so that it points at a star or planet, the user can measure its angle from the horizon. The astrolabe has many other uses.

An Earth-centered model of the Universe could never quite match the real movements of the planets. In the early 1500s, a Polish astronomer named Nicolaus Copernicus revived the idea of a Sun-centered Universe, but it took time to perfect his model.

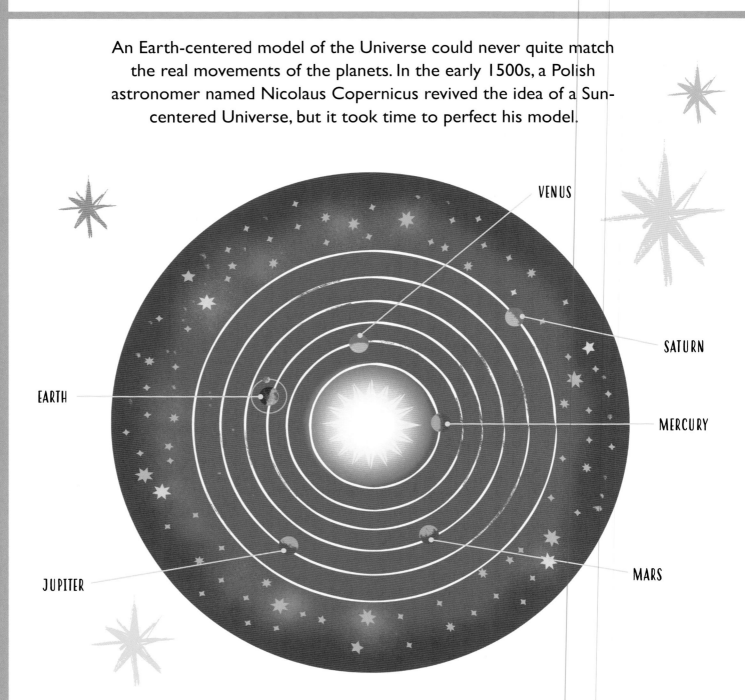

Copernicus said that Earth was the third planet from the Sun, with the Moon in orbit around it. Mercury and Venus orbited closer in, which was why they always appeared near the Sun in Earth's skies. Mars, Jupiter, and Saturn lay further out, and made loops in the sky when Earth passed between them and the Sun.

Copernicus placed all of the planets on circular orbits, moving at steady rates around the Sun. Unfortunately, he soon found that his model was no better than the Earth-centered one at predicting the actual movements of planets, so he had to add a system of epicycles similar to Ptolemy's.

KEPLER'S LAWS

In the early 1600s, German mathematician Johannes Kepler took a fresh look at the motion of planets, based on precise records of the movement of Mars. He realized that the orbits of the planets were elongated ellipses rather than perfect circles, and he outlined three laws of planetary motion.

First Law

Planets orbit following ellipses (circles stretched in one direction), with the Sun at one of two focus points on either side of the center. A circle is just a special type of ellipse with both focus points at the exact center.

Second Law

A planet moves more slowly when it is further from the Sun, and faster when it is closer to the Sun. A line between the Sun and a planet "sweeps out" equal areas in equal times.

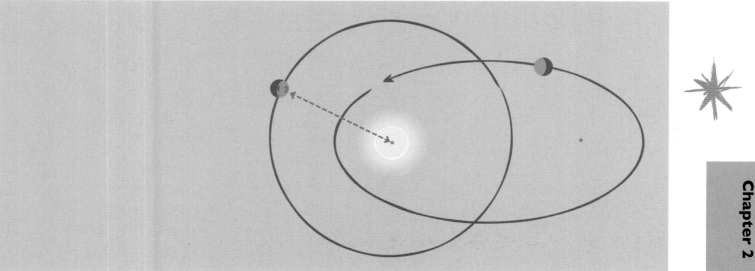

GALILEO'S DISCOVERIES

Italian scientist Galileo Galilei was one of the first people to look at the sky through a telescope. It led him to a series of discoveries that convinced him that Copernicus was right—the Sun really did sit in the middle of the solar system.

GALILEO'S TELESCOPES

The telescope was invented by Hans Lippershey, a lensmaker in Holland, around 1608. Italian astronomer Galileo Galilei built his own versions and used them to study the sky. Within a few years, he had improved their magnification from three times to 30 times the size of an object. Galileo didn't just use his telescopes to look at the sky. He also tried to sell them to traders, so that they could spot which cargo ships were coming into port before anyone else.

A NEW LOOK AT THE SKY

Galileo's telescopes showed him objects that are too faint or have details too small to see with the unaided eye.

Moons of Jupiter

When he looked at Jupiter, he saw that it was a disk, with four smaller "stars" in a line around it. As he watched these stars move back and forth, he realized they were moons circling Jupiter. This showed that not everything in the Universe orbited around Earth or the Sun.

Phases of Venus

When Galileo looked at Venus, the brightest planet in the sky, he found that it went through a series of Moon-like **phases**. These showed that it was orbiting the Sun and changing its appearance depending on how much of its sunlit face was visible from Earth.

Mountains on the Moon

Looking at the surface of the Moon, Galileo saw mountains, craters, and dark plains he called "seas." Earlier astronomers had believed that the Moon and Sun were perfect spheres, but these discoveries showed that it was a rugged world like Earth.

GALILEO ON TRIAL

Galileo revealed these discoveries and others in a book called *The Starry Messenger*. He became a strong supporter of Copernicus's ideas, but because the Catholic Church supported Ptolemy's Earth-centered Universe, this got him into trouble. He spent the last years of his life under house arrest, but he is now regarded as a hero of science.

GREAT TELESCOPES

YEAR	TELESCOPE	
1609	Galileo's refractor	First telescope used to observe the night sky
1668	Newton's reflector	First mirror-based telescope design
1673	Hevelius' aerial telescope	Had a 20 cm (8 in) lens, requiring a 46-m (150-ft)-long frame
1845	Leviathan of Parsonstown	First giant mirror telescope, with a 1.83 m (72 in) diameter
1897	Yerkes Refractor	Largest lens-based telescope, with a 1.02 m (40 in) diameter
1948	Hale Telescope	5 m (16 ft) mirror telescope
1990	Hubble Space Telescope	First large visible light telescope in orbit
2009	Gran Telescopio Canarias	World's largest single telescope, with a 10.4 m (410 in) mirror
2027	Extremely Large Telescope	Giant telescope with a 39.3 m (129 ft) mirror

Before the 1800s, astronomers were mostly interested in measuring the positions and movements of the stars and planets. With this in mind, they built elaborate observatories and compiled their measurements in beautiful star atlases.

THE AGE OF OBSERVATORIES

Observatories are special buildings designed to house and protect telescopes and other astronomical instruments. Having these instruments fixed in place and correctly lined up with the sky was key to accurately measuring the position of stars.

Polish astronomer Johannes Hevelius built an observatory platform spanning three rooftops in the city of Gdańsk. His instruments included devices for measuring the precise positions of stars and planets, as well as a telescope with a tube some 46 m (150 ft) long to get the best magnification.

HEVELIUS' ATLAS

The invention of telescopes meant that astronomers could see many more stars and other objects. Making accurate maps of their locations became increasingly important, and many astronomers in the 1700s set out to make elaborate star atlases. One of the most important was made by Hevelius and published in 1687.

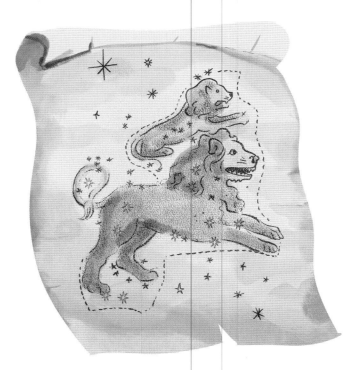

THE HERSCHELS' DISCOVERIES

In the late 1800s, William Herschel, a German musician living in Bath, England, built reflecting telescopes that were far superior to any previous instrument. William and his sister, Caroline, used these to make important discoveries that transformed our understanding of the solar system and beyond.

New Planets

In 1781, William Herschel was charting the stars when he discovered what at first he thought was a new comet. It turned out to be something far more important—a new planet, which was later named "Uranus." By the 1840s, astronomers realized that Uranus's movement was being influenced by another unseen world, which led to the discovery of the outermost major planet, Neptune.

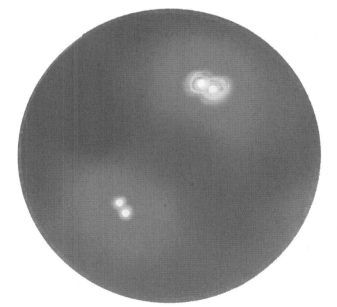

Double Stars

Herschel discovered that many stars that looked like single objects at first, were actually close pairs when seen through a telescope. He showed that these couldn't all be chance alignments—instead, the double stars must be genuine pairs in orbit around each other.

OUT OF CURIOSITY

In a time when clocks were not reliable, the sky was the only accurate way of figuring out both the time and a stargazer's position on Earth. People hoped that more precise maps and a better understanding of how the planets moved could be the key to safe and accurate navigation of ships.

THE BIRTH OF ASTROPHYSICS

Beginning in the 1800s, astronomers learned how to measure the properties of stars—their temperatures, sizes, masses, and even the chemicals they contained. This allowed them to unlock the secrets of how the stars shine.

Apart from the Sun, every star in the sky is so far away that it appears as just a point of light through even the most powerful telescopes. By measuring the distance to stars for the first time, astronomers were able to discover their true **luminosities**—the amount of energy that they pump out as light. When they realized that a star's color was related to its surface temperature, they had the key to calculating the size of stars. They discovered that stars vary hugely in luminosity, temperature, and size.

Red dwarfs are small, faint stars with about half the mass of the Sun or less. They have comparatively cool surfaces that glow red. The faintest may be a million times dimmer than the Sun.

Stars like the Sun are known as **yellow dwarfs**—they have moderate brightness and their surfaces glow yellow.

Stars with a few times the mass of the Sun are inflated by the energy of their escaping radiation and have hot surfaces that glow blue-white.

Supergiants are rare and incredibly luminous stars. They may have the mass of many Suns and pump out a million times its energy, sometimes shining with intense blue light.

STELLAR CHEMISTRY

From the 1890s onward, a group of female astronomers at Harvard College Observatory in the United States measured the rainbow-like **spectra** created by splitting up starlight according to its energy and color. Patterns they found in the spectra showed when various elements were present, and they also revealed the stars' temperature and other properties.

WEIGHING THE STARS

After astronomers discovered that some stars form pairs orbiting each other, they had a way of comparing their masses—the lighter star has a bigger orbit, while the heavier one moves less and is closer to the system's balance point or "center of mass." Comparing the masses of stars with their color, size, and luminosity revealed important patterns.

THE POWER SOURCE OF STARS

In 1920, British astronomer Arthur Eddington suggested that the stars might be powered by **nuclear fusion**, forcing together lightweight elements to form heavier

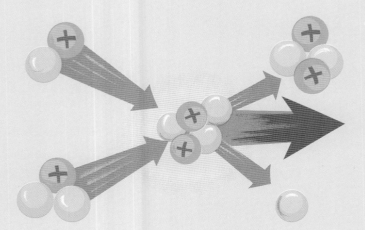

ones and release energy. This theory explained the huge difference in the luminosity of stars. A small difference in mass can make a big difference to the rate at which fusion reactions take place and the total amount of energy that the star can pump out.

THE EXPANDING UNIVERSE

Until the early twentieth century, most astronomers thought that everything in the sky lay inside our galaxy. Then, they discovered that not only were there countless other galaxies beyond our own, but the Universe is expanding.

In the mid 1800s, powerful new telescopes revealed that some **nebulae** (fuzzy, cloudlike objects in the night sky) seemed to be made not of gas, but of large numbers of stars, often in a spiral shape. At the time, no one knew that the Milky Way was itself a spiral, but astronomers still argued over whether the "spiral nebulae" were fairly small objects in nearby space or much bigger and farther away—separate galaxies similar in size to the Milky Way itself.

In 1920, astronomers Heber D. Curtis and Harlow Shapley argued the case for and against other galaxies. Shapley said that if the spiral nebulae were really far away, they'd have to be truly enormous objects—much larger than anything people of the time had imagined. Curtis discovered that most spiral nebulae were moving at far higher speeds than stars in the Milky Way, suggesting that they might be a different kind of object.

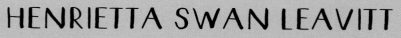

HENRIETTA SWAN LEAVITT

In 1908, Henrietta Swan Leavitt discovered a special type of star with regular changes in brightness that happen more quickly if the star is brighter. Knowing the true brightness of these stars meant that astronomers could calculate their distances. In 1925, Edwin Hubble found variable stars of this type in some of the spiral nebulae. They confirmed that the spirals lay far outside the Milky Way.

THE BLOW-UP UNIVERSE

In 1929, Hubble compared the distances of the spiral galaxies to the speed at which they moved. This revealed that the greater a galaxy's distance from the Milky Way, the faster it tends to be moving away from us. This isn't because the Milky Way is "unpopular"— the same applies to every other galaxy, because the space between them is expanding.

The Universe as a whole is expanding like a balloon, pulling the galaxies within it apart. The more space there is between galaxies, the faster the gap between them expands.

The idea that the Universe today is rapidly expanding raises an obvious question—was it ever compressed together in one place? This is the idea behind the **Big Bang theory**, our best explanation for the origin of the Universe.

INTO THE SPACE AGE

When the first rockets reached outer space in the 1950s, it opened up new opportunities for astronomy. Orbital telescopes offer clearer views of deep space and let astronomers collect signals that never reach our planet's surface.

Earth is surrounded by an atmosphere of gases that get thinner the higher you go. Moving air in Earth's lower atmosphere can act like a glass lens, distorting the paths of light rays so that even the largest telescopes see blurry images.

Getting above the atmosphere, using either a telescope on a spacecraft or a satellite that enters a permanent orbit around the Earth, allows a much clearer view of the Universe. What's more, a telescope in orbit can always point away from the Sun, so daylight doesn't interfere with viewing. It can look at the night sky 24 hours a day, seven days a week.

OUT OF CURIOSITY

According to the FAI, an organization that keeps records of flying and spaceflight achievements, outer space begins 100 km (62 mi) above Earth's surface. US space agency NASA, however, disagrees and says it starts at 80 km (50 mi).

THE ELECTROMAGNETIC SPECTRUM

Light is an **electromagnetic** (EM) wave. Eletromagnetism is when forces occur between electrically charged particles to produce energy. Stars and other space objects produce EM waves with a huge range of different energies and wavelengths (the distance separating peaks or troughs of the ripple), but only a few can make it through Earth's atmosphere. These include visible light and some long-wavelength radio waves.

EYES ACROSS THE SPECTRUM

Telescopes have to be specially designed to capture radiation with longer or shorter waves than everyday light.

Radio waves: Many very long EM waves reach Earth's surface, but radio telescopes need to be huge in order to make images from waves with such long wavelengths. Huge metal reflector dishes (up to 100 m or 330 ft across) focus waves onto a receiver and build up pictures by measuring how the radio wave strength changes as they scan slowly across the sky.

Infrared: Infrared is often called "heat radiation". It allows us to see objects that do not shine with visible light. Infrared telescopes are cooled to very low temperatures, so their own warmth doesn't drown out the signal.

Visible light: Our eyes have evolved to see a narrow range of EM waves. Our brains interpret different wavelengths of light as different colors. Earth's atmosphere is mostly transparent to visible light, but telescopes such as the Hubble Space Telescope can still get clearer views of the Universe.

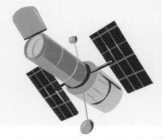

Ultraviolet: These waves carry more energy than normal light. Stars hotter than the Sun give off most of their energy as ultraviolet waves, but these are blocked by Earth's atmosphere, so they have to be observed with space-based telescopes.

X-rays: These waves have very high energies and come from million-degree gas clouds in space. They pass straight through normal mirrors, so X-ray telescopes have shallow metal surfaces that make the rays ricochet onto a detector.

Gamma rays: The shortest EM waves are produced by violent events in the distant Universe, such as the formation of black holes. Gamma-ray telescopes use clever designs to detect rays passing through them and calculate the direction they came from.

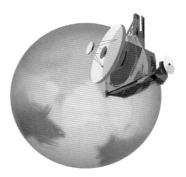

CHAPTER 3

DISCOVERING THE SOLAR SYSTEM

The solar system is the region of space dominated by the Sun and everything within it. This includes not just the eight planets, their moons and rings, but also countless smaller objects that orbit among them, such as rocky asteroids and icy comets.

In this chapter, we'll take a close look at the Moon and the many planets spinning around our Sun, and at how humankind has used technology to explore these distant worlds.

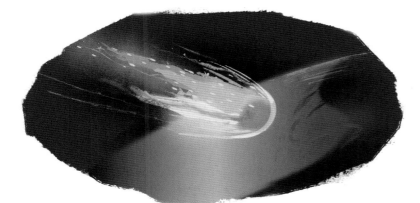

OBSERVING THE MOON

The Moon is Earth's only natural satellite—a huge ball of rock orbiting around 400,000 km (250,000 miles) away. This closeness to Earth means you can easily see details on the lunar surface and pick out lots of detail with binoculars or a telescope.

MOON MAP

The Moon has two main types of terrain—dark plains called "seas," where there are few craters, and bright "highlands" covered in craters. The surface has been bombarded with space rocks throughout its history, which have carved out craters of all sizes. This bombardment was at its heaviest up to 3.8 billion years ago. Three billion years ago, changes inside the Moon caused molten lava to erupt through cracks in the surface, flooding the largest craters. The lava set into solid rock to create dark lunar seas.

PLATO CRATER

SEA OF COLD

ARISTARCHUS CRATER

SEA OF RAIN

ARCHIMEDES CRATER

SEA OF SERENITY

KEPLER CRATER

COPERNICUS CRATER

OCEAN OF STORMS

SEA OF VAPOR

SEA OF CRISES

SEA OF ISLANDS

SEA OF TRANQUILITY

SEA OF FERTILITY

SEA OF MOISTURE

SEA OF CLOUDS

SEA OF NECTAR

TYCHO CRATER

MOON PHASES

The Moon orbits Earth every 27.3 days and turns on its **axis** at the exact same time, so that the same side is always facing Earth. As different amounts of the Earth-facing surface are lit by the Sun, it goes through a series of phases, from new Moon to full Moon and back.

Because the Sun's direction from Earth is also changing, it actually takes 29.5 days for the Moon to return to the same phase as the previous month.

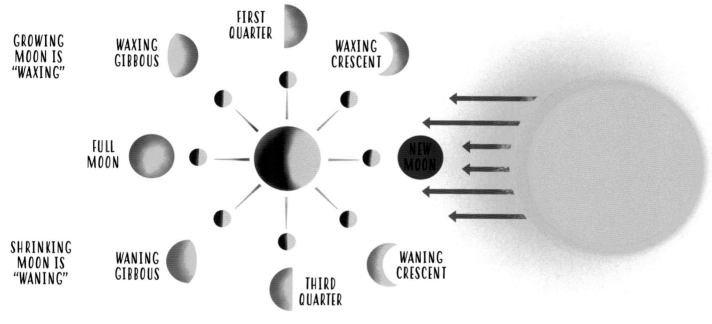

GROWING MOON IS "WAXING"

WAXING GIBBOUS

FIRST QUARTER

WAXING CRESCENT

FULL MOON

NEW MOON

SHRINKING MOON IS "WANING"

WANING GIBBOUS

THIRD QUARTER

WANING CRESCENT

OUT OF CURIOSITY

Rock samples brought back by astronauts show that the Moon's rocks are similar—but not identical—to Earth's. The Moon is also very large compared to the size of Earth itself; most moons are much smaller than their parent planets. Most astronomers now think that the Moon formed when a Mars-sized rogue planet struck Earth about 4.5 billion years ago. It threw a huge fountain of molten rock into orbit, where it came together into a new satellite.

THE FAR SIDE

Space probe photos show that the far side of the Moon has far fewer dark seas—this is because most of the volcanic eruptions happened on the Earth-facing side.

MOSCOW SEA

TSIOLKOVSKY CRATER

INVESTIGATING THE SUN

The Sun is the star at the center of our solar system—a huge ball of gas generating energy that provides light and heat to the planets and other objects in its orbit.

The Sun's interior is made up of gas that gets denser (more tightly packed) and hotter toward a core where temperatures can reach 15 million °C (27 million °F). Energy pushing out from the core creates two more distinct internal layers, before finally escaping into space at the **photosphere**, the Sun's upper layer where its gas becomes mostly transparent.

In the Sun's core, hydrogen gas is forced together to make helium and release energy as gamma rays.

Prominences are loops of cool gas running high above the surface, created by the Sun's tangled magnetic field.

At the base of the convective layer, the Sun's gas changes. It absorbs energy from below as heat, which sends it rising up like hot air.

Solar flares are bursts of energy released when prominences collapse.

At the photosphere, the hot gas releases energy again in the form of light and heat that escape into space.

Sunspots are dark markings on the surface where the photosphere is cooler.

Gamma rays escaping from the core bounce back and forth in the foggy radiative layer, taking tens of thousands of years to move outward.

SOLAR ECLIPSES

Solar eclipses happen on rare occasions when the Moon passes across the face of the Sun as seen from Earth.

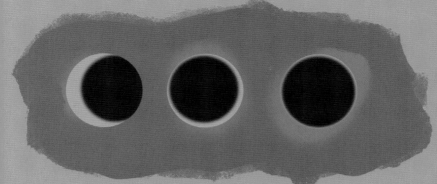

Partial eclipse:
The Moon partially blocks the Sun—look for strange-shaped shadows on the ground.

Total eclipse:
The Moon blocks light from the photosphere completely. For a few minutes, much fainter light from the Sun's outer atmosphere, or **corona**, becomes visible.

Annular eclipse: The Moon passes right in front of the Sun, but because it's at its farthest from Earth, a ring of sunlight shines around it.

SOLAR PROJECTION

The Sun's light is so bright that it can easily damage your eyes, so you should never look at it directly. The best way to see features on the Sun is by using a telescope or binoculars (with one of the two large lenses covered by its cap) to project the Sun's image onto a card or paper screen. You can see the Sun's shape during a partial eclipse and also track changing patterns of sunspots.

- Professional astronomers use special telescopes that block nearly all of the Sun's light and only allow a very small amount through to reveal surface details. Safety-graded "eclipse glasses" do a similar job, so you can look at the Sun during a partial eclipse.

OUT OF CURIOSITY
Astronomers can measure the Sun's rotation by tracking how sunspots change their location on its disk. Their results show that the Sun isn't solid—at the equator, it spins in about 25 days, but near the poles it takes around 35!

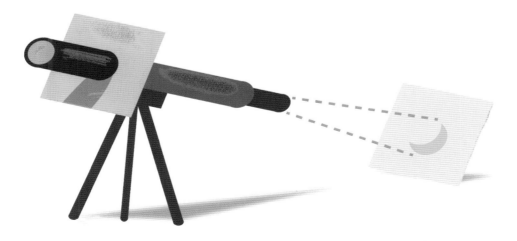

👓 STUDYING THE PLANETS 👓

The five closest planets to Earth are all visible with the naked eye if you know where to look. Track them from week to week to study their movements, or use binoculars or a small telescope to see some of their most interesting features.

👓 INFERIOR PLANETS

Mercury and Venus both orbit closer to the Sun than Earth—they are called inferior planets, and their movements are confined to loops around the Sun. Mercury, the smallest and innermost planet, is usually lost in its glare. It can only be spotted for a few days at dawn or dusk, when it is at its farthest from the Sun. Venus can get much farther away from the Sun and spend months in dark evening or early morning skies, when it often outshines everything except the Moon.

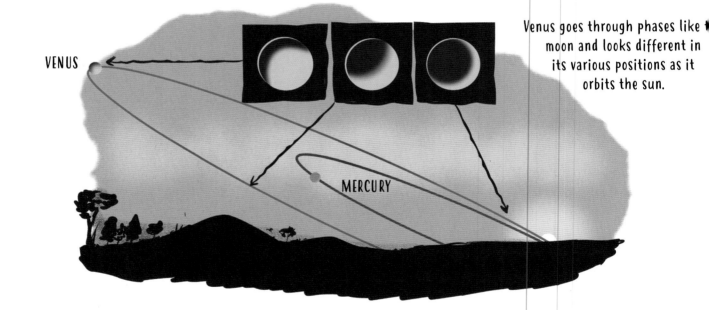

VENUS

MERCURY

Venus goes through phases like the moon and looks different in its various positions as it orbits the sun.

Planets with phases

The distance from Earth to Mercury and Venus varies depending on how the planets are arranged. At **superior conjunction**, they are on the opposite side of the Sun to Earth, while at **inferior conjunction**, they are on the near side and closest to Earth. Both planets go through a cycle of phases like the Moon, depending on how much of the sunlit side we can see. Mercury is so small that its phases are hard to spot, but Venus's are easily seen through binoculars or a small telescope—especially when it is a thin crescent.

👓 SUPERIOR PLANETS

Mars, Jupiter, and Saturn are the three naked-eye "superior" planets, orbiting the Sun farther out than Earth. This means they can make circles all the way around the sky, appearing at their biggest and brightest at "opposition," when they are directly opposite the Sun, and rise as it sets.

Features on Mars

Mars can go from big and bright to small and faint, but it's easy to find thanks to its orange-red color. At its brightest, a telescope can show dark plains on its surface, and gleaming white ice caps at the poles, which change in size depending on the Martian seasons.

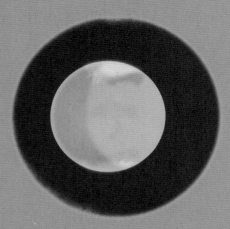

Jupiter's moons and clouds

Jupiter is the largest planet in the solar system and is much farther away than Mars, so the arrangement of planets doesn't affect its brightness as much. Binoculars will show Jupiter's four giant moons shifting from side to side of the bright disk from one night to the next. Even a small telescope will show some of the dark cloud bands that wrap around the planet.

Rings of Saturn

Saturn is smaller than Jupiter and almost twice as far away. It looks like a yellowish "star" that takes nearly 30 years to circle through the zodiac constellations. Binoculars will show something strange about its shape, but it takes a telescope to really see the shape of its rings.

- The angle of Saturn's rings to Earth changes through each orbit. Sometimes they are side-on, but every 15 years they lie edge-on to Earth and nearly disappear from sight.

FRAGMENTS OF THE SOLAR SYSTEM

The space between the planets is mostly empty, but there are plenty of small objects following their own paths around the Sun. These vary from dust clouds to space rocks that pass through Earth's atmosphere.

SHOOTING STARS

Most of the small objects that cross Earth's path through space are tiny specks of dust. As they plunge into the thin gas of the outer atmosphere, they heat them up due top friction from the air, and they burn away in short-lived trails of light known as shooting stars or **meteors**.

METEOR STREAMS

Meteors enter the atmosphere from different directions all the time, but sometimes Earth meets a large cloud of dust on its own path through space, such as that left behind the orbit of a **comet**. When Earth runs into one of these "meteor streams," the result is a shower of shooting stars coming from one direction. They appear to radiate from a point in the sky.

ANNUAL SHOWERS

Because Earth crosses some meteor streams at the same time each year, they can be predicted. Here are some of the brightest and best known.

Most of these showers take place over several nights on either side of their peak.

NAME	CONSTELLATION	PEAK AROUND	PEAK METEORS PER HOUR
Quadrantids	Boötes	January 4	110
Lyrids	Lyra	April 23	18
Eta Aquariids	Aquarius	May 6	50
Delta Aquariids	Aquarius	July 30	25
Perseids	Perseus	August 12	100
Orionids	Orion	October 21	25
Leonids	Leo	November 17	10 (but storms of thousands happen about every 33 years)
Geminids	Gemini	December 15	150

METEORITES

On rare occasions, chunks of solid rock fall into Earth's atmosphere. These objects can create spectacular fireballs called **bolides** as they fall. Friction with the air can slow them down, and sometimes they can even survive to hit the ground. They are then known as **meteorites**.

Meteorites allow scientists to study fragments of other worlds in laboratories on Earth. Some come from the Moon and some from Mars, but most are chunks of asteroids that may have changed little since the early days of the solar system.

OUT OF CURIOSITY

While some meteorites stand out from their surroundings, others blend in and are hard to tell from Earth rocks. One way to track down meteorites is to look in places with no natural rocks, such as ice sheets or deserts; any rocks found there must have fallen out of the sky!

IMPACT CRATERS

When large meteorites hit the ground, the results can be spectacular—a shock wave melts both the meteorite and the rock below, spraying it over the nearby landscape and forming a bowl-shaped impact crater. On Earth, these craters are rapidly worn down and disguised, but many other worlds in the solar system preserve countless impact craters from their ancient history.

DINO EXTINCTION

Around 66 million years ago, a 10-km (6-mile) chunk of space rock struck what is now Mexico. The aftermath of the impact, including huge tidal waves, wildfires, and years of dark, cold skies around the world, brought an end to the age of the dinosaurs.

EXPLORERS ON THE MOON

The Moon may be the closest world to Earth, but visiting still requires crossing 400,000 km (250,000 miles) of space, then surviving hostile conditions on the lunar surface.

ROBOT PIONEERS

When humans set the goal of reaching the Moon in the 1960s, we'd only ever seen it from a distance. Space probes (unmanned devices sent to explore space) were launched to learn more about conditions before a landing could be planned.

Robot probes included the Lunar Orbiter which mapped the surface from a distance, the Ranger (right) which sent back close-up pictures before smashing into the surface, and the Surveyors which sent back data about surface conditions.

- **Until the first Surveyor landings, many scientists worried that the Moon's surface was a sea of dust that would swallow up anything that landed on it.**

TO THE MOON AND BACK

In order to reach the Moon, engineers at US space agency NASA came up with an ingenious plan. A giant rocket launched a three-part spacecraft named Apollo toward the Moon. One part (the Lunar Module) was designed to land on the surface, while another (the linked Command and Service Modules) kept a third astronaut in orbit around the Moon. All three astronauts traveled home to Earth in the third part, the Command Module.

WALKING ON THE MOON

The Apollo Lunar Module carried two astronauts to the lunar surface, while a third remained in the orbiting Command Module. Astronauts wore spacesuits to shield them from the airless conditions and extreme temperatures, with thick boots and multiple layers to protect them from sharp moon rocks. The Apollo 11 mission was the first to land people on the moon, but five successful Apollo missions followed. The last three missions also carried an electric car called the Lunar Roving Vehicle.

LUNAR MODULE

The Lunar Module had a crew cabin mounted on a spiderlike landing section. Rockets in the landing section fired to steer the module's descent. When the surface expedition ended, a separate rocket underneath the crew cabin fired to blast it free of the landing section and return it to lunar orbit.

THE APOLLO LANDINGS

NAME	LUNAR MODULE	LANDING DATE	LANDING SITE	EXPEDITION LENGTH
Apollo 11	Eagle	July 1969	Sea of Tranquillity	21 hours
Apollo 12	Intrepid	November 1969	Ocean of Storms	32 hours
Apollo 14	Antares	February 1971	Fra Mauro region	33 hours
Apollo 15	Falcon	July 1971	Apennine mountains	67 hours
Apollo 16	Orion	April 1971	Descartes highlands	71 hours
Apollo 17	Challenger	December 1972	Taurus–Littrow valley	75 hours

OUT OF CURIOSITY

The Apollo missions brought 382 kg (842 lb) of rock samples from the surface of the Moon. Unlike Earth, the Moon's airless surface doesn't change, so it preserves a record of everything that happened in its history. By studying the Apollo rocks in labs on Earth, scientists have been able to build up a history not just of the Moon, but of major events in the history of the entire solar system.

FLYBYS AND ORBITERS

We've learned a lot about the bodies in our solar system by sending robot spacecraft to visit them. These space probes either fly past another world at high speed (flybys), or enter orbit and sometimes land on a planet or moon to conduct a long-term study.

GRAND TOURISTS

The space between the planets is vast, and because planets move at different speeds, the best routes to reach them are constantly changing. In the 1970s, NASA built two Voyager space probes to take advantage of a rare arrangement of the giant planets that would allow a spacecraft to visit each of the four outer worlds in turn on a so-called "Grand Tour."

VOYAGER 2 FLEW PAST JUPITER AND SATURN, THEN CONTINUED TO URANUS AND NEPTUNE.

VOYAGER 1 FLEW PAST JUPITER AND SATURN BEFORE HEADING INTO INTERSTELLAR SPACE.

OUT OF CURIOSITY
The Voyagers and some other space probes made use of a clever trick called a slingshot or "gravity assist." By flying toward one planet, they were pulled in by its gravity and sped up. Then, a carefully timed change of direction allowed them to break free and fly on to their next destination at a higher speed.

PARKER SOLAR PROBE AND SUN

The Parker Solar Probe, launched in 2018, is built to withstand searing temperatures as it flies through the Sun's outer atmosphere. A heat shield protects the body of the spacecraft from direct sunlight, with only a couple of instruments peaking out from behind it—the probe gathers most of its information by analyzing the conditions it meets along its flight path.

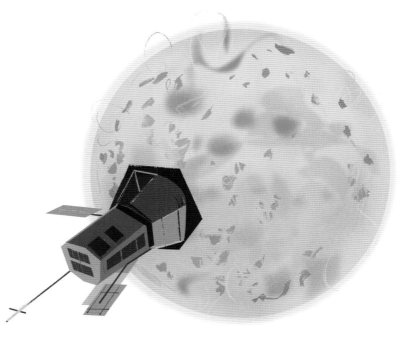

NEW HORIZONS

In 2006, New Horizons set a record for the fastest spacecraft ever launched from Earth. Traveling at 58,500 km/h (36,400 mph), this stripped-down probe picked up even more speed during a flyby of Jupiter, before hurtling past the dwarf planet Pluto—34 times farther from the Sun than Earth—in 2015.

KEY FLYBY AND ORBITER MISSIONS

PROBE	LAUNCHED	ACHIEVEMENTS
Luna 3	1959	Flyby returned images of the far side of the Moon
Luna 12	1966	First images of the Moon from orbit
Mariner 9	1971	First spacecraft to orbit Mars
Galileo	1989	Seven-year survey of Jupiter and its moons
Cassini	1995	Thirteen-year survey of the Saturn system
Rosetta	2004	Orbited and touched down on comet 67P
Messenger	2004	First probe to orbit Mercury
Dawn	2007	Orbited the asteroids Vesta and Ceres

LANDERS AND ROVERS

Spacecraft that land on alien worlds can reveal a huge amount about surface conditions, but making a landing on another planet or moon, then sending data back to Earth, requires ingenious engineering.

HUYGENS TITAN PROBE

The shield-shaped Huygens probe hitched a ride to Saturn aboard the bus-sized Cassini orbiter, then detached and parachuted into the thick atmosphere of the giant moon Titan. Data it sent back to Cassini revealed a chilly surface temperature of -179 °C (-290 °F).

VENERA 13

From the 1960s to the 1980s, a series of Russian Venera probes attempted to land on Venus. Early missions reported searing temperatures and crushing pressure from the atmosphere, so later landers were built to withstand hostile conditions. Even then, they could only survive for a few minutes, returning images of the planet's baking volcanic landscape.

🪂 PERSEVERANCE MARS ROVER

Mars is the planet in the solar system most like Earth—and the one with the most successful landings. As well as probes designed for specific studies, five wheeled rovers have explored the surface, photographing their surroundings and collecting and studying rock samples to provide information on Martian history.

The Perseverance rover landed on Mars in 2021. Its six wheels have independent motors and suspension that allows the rover to cross rough terrain, while cameras on a central pillar view the landscape in 3D and analyze the makeup of nearby rocks. The rover's robot arm carries a drill for collecting samples, which can be tested in an onboard laboratory.

🪂 MARS LANDERS

Viking 1	1976	Lander with onboard laboratory
Viking 2	1976	Lander with onboard laboratory
Mars Pathfinder/Sojourner	1997	Lander with small test rover
Spirit	2004	Rover
Opportunity	2004	Rover
Phoenix	2008	Polar lander
Curiosity	2012	Advanced rover
Insight	2018	Lander with instruments to study interior of Mars
Tianwen-1/Zhurong	2021	Lander and rover
Perseverance	2021	Advanced rover

MINOR PLANETS

Many small worlds orbit the Sun between and beyond the major planets.
They include rocky asteroids (mostly between Mars and Jupiter) and icy
Kuiper Belt Objects (KBOs) beyond the orbit of Neptune.

GAPS IN THE SOLAR SYSTEM

In the early 1800s, after the discovery of Uranus, astronomers noticed a pattern in the orbits of the planets with what seemed to be a large gap between Mars and Jupiter. When they scoured this part of space looking for a missing planet, they found the first objects in the **asteroid** belt.

Later, astronomers wondered if the orbits of both Uranus and Neptune were being affected by the gravity of an unknown planet even farther from the Sun. In 1930, they discovered Pluto in an orbit beyond Neptune. It is too small to influence the planets closest to it, but it turned out to be the first known member of the Kuiper belt.

* **Some "Near-Earth Asteroids" have orbits that cross between the rocky planets, while some icy objects called centaurs weave between the giant planets.**

OUT OF CURIOSITY
The cloud of material that formed the solar system was made from a mix of rocky and icy materials, but as the newborn Sun got hotter, it turned most of the ice inside the orbit of Jupiter into gassy vapor. The solar wind (streams of tiny high-speed particles blowing out from the Sun) pushed this vapor out of the inner solar system, leaving only the rocky materials behind to form the planets and asteroids. Farther out, the ice survived long enough to come together in larger objects.

DWARF PLANETS

Astronomers call both Ceres (the largest asteroid) and Pluto (the largest known KBO) **dwarf planets**. They have some of the features of planets, such as a spherical shape, but don't have enough gravity to affect the orbits of smaller objects passing nearby in the same way as major planets.

ASTEROIDS

CERES

PLUTO

THE MOON

- Three other Kuiper Belt Objects named Eris, Haumea, and Makemake have so far passed the shape test to count as dwarf planets, but most astronomers think there are many more still to find.

INSIDE ASTEROIDS

Inside some large asteroids, heavy materials sink to the middle and create a layered structure similar to the inside of a planet. If the asteroid breaks up in a collision, this can create smaller asteroids of different types.

When gravity pulls together smaller fragments at slow speeds, they can stick together to form a "rubble pile" asteroid, with large gaps hidden inside. Over millions of years, bombardment by space dust breaks up the surface into a smooth, powdered rock known as "breccia."

ASTEROID MINING

Asteroids contain most of the same elements that formed Earth, but because they haven't been altered by chemical reactions in the past four billion years, they should be much easier to extract. This is why several companies are making plans to mine small asteroids. They say this could produce cheaper materials—with less environmental damage—than mining on Earth.

VISITORS FROM THE EDGE

Comets are icy objects from the edge of the solar system that sometimes fall into orbits that bring them closer to the Sun. As their ice melts, they develop a head called a coma and a tail that may be millions of miles long.

COMET ORBITS

Comets that enter the inner solar system follow extremely stretched elliptical orbits that come very close to the Sun at one end. As the comet approaches the Sun, it picks up speed and develops its tail, which is blown by the **solar wind** of particles streaming from the Sun. This is why, even as the comet swings around the Sun and begins to retreat, its tail always points away from the Sun.

COMET TYPES

Sungrazer: These comets get so close to the Sun that they often break up or melt completely.

Short-period: These comets take fewer than 200 years to orbit the Sun. They get fainter with age as they lose ice on each return to the Sun.

Long-period: These unpredictable comets may take thousands of years to orbit or visit the Sun only once, but they can be truly spectacular.

WHERE COMETS COME FROM

Most comets orbit the Sun in a vast spherical shell called the **Oort Cloud**. This cloud's outer reaches are a quarter of the way to the nearest stars. Occasional collisions or close encounters between comets send them tumbling toward the inner solar system.

COMET STRUCTURE

A comet's icy nucleus is usually just a few miles across and is coated in very dark sooty chemicals. When it gets heated up by the Sun, ice beneath the crust begins to melt, and jets of vapor burst out to form a thin but vast atmosphere called the **coma**. Some of this gas is swept away by the solar wind as a bluish, electrically charged "ion tail" that points away from the Sun. Rocky material blowing out with the gas forms a second yellowish tail that bends back along the comet's orbit. This is called a "dust tail."

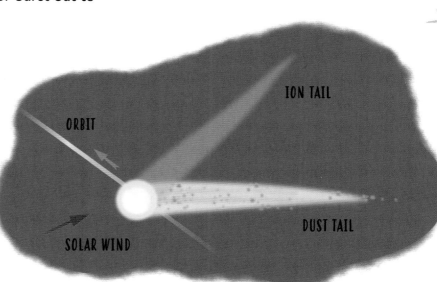

ION TAIL

ORBIT

DUST TAIL

SOLAR WIND

OUT OF CURIOSITY

Halley's Comet is the best known and one of the brightest short-period comets. It orbits the Sun every 76 years and has been traced back to at least 240 BCE. In 1066, it was seen shortly before the Norman invasion of England and is depicted on the famous Bayeux Tapestry. It was last seen in 1986 and will return again in 2061.

CHAPTER 4

SECRETS OF THE STARS

Nearly all the lights you see in the night sky are stars—distant objects that shine like the Sun and can be seen across vast expanses of space.

In this chapter, we'll find out how stars are born and how they die. We'll also compare the different types of stars, from red dwarfs to blue supergiants, and explore mysterious black holes.

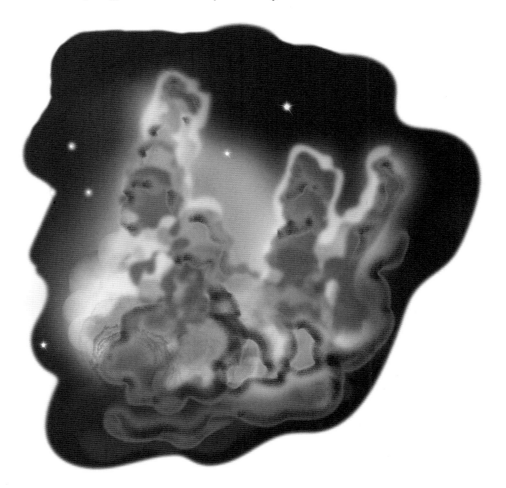

WHAT IS A STAR?

Not all stars are the same. Some are bright, some are faint, some are brilliant white, and others a dull red. There are even stars that change their brightness over periods of hours or months. Stars vary hugely in their size, distance from Earth, energy output, and other properties.

COSMIC FIREBALLS

Stars, including our Sun, are enormous balls of gas in space, with cores that get so hot and dense that they can generate their own energy. This prevents stars from collapsing completely under their own mass, and also makes them the main source of light in the Universe.

OUT OF CURIOSITY

Often you'll notice that the brightest stars in the sky are constantly twinkling. This is because the moving air in Earth's atmosphere acts like a shifting lens that distorts the star's light rays and bounces them in various directions. Stars are affected by twinkling because of their vast distance from Earth. The planets in our solar system are much closer and their reflected light arrives on Earth in a much wider beam, so they twinkle much less.

⭐ CLOSEST AND BRIGHTEST

The closest star to our solar system, Proxima Centauri, is so faint that you can only see it with a telescope. It pumps out less than 1/600th of the light of the Sun. The brightest star in the sky, Sirius, is twice as far away as Proxima, but shines brilliantly because it is 25 times more luminous than the Sun.

PROXIMA

THE SUN

SIRIUS

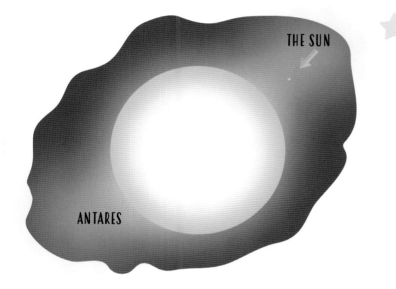

THE SUN

ANTARES

⭐ STARS BIG AND SMALL

Despite being 1.4 million km (870,000 miles) across, the Sun is on the small side for a star. The largest stars of all, the **supergiants**, can grow to 1 billion km (620 million miles) across or more. If the red supergiant Antares was in the middle of our solar system, its outer layers would stretch almost to Jupiter. Stars with larger surfaces have more space to shed the energy they generate inside. This means that less energy passes through each unit of surface area and its surface is cooler.

⭐ STELLAR DISTANCES

If the solar system between the Sun and Saturn was scaled down to the size of this page, you'd have to keep going for 28,047 times the distance from the Sun to Saturn to reach the nearest star. Distances to stars are so vast that astronomers use a huge unit called a **light year** to measure them. A light year is the distance light (the fastest thing in the Universe) travels in one year. One light year is 63,241 times the distance from the Earth to the Sun. That's 9.5 trillion km (5.9 trillion miles). Proxima Centauri is 4.25 light years away, but most stars are even more distant.

MEASURING THE STARS

To understand what stars are, astronomers need to measure their various properties. The most important of these are brightness (as seen from Earth), temperature, and distance.

⭐ BRIGHTNESS OF STARS

Astronomers measure the brightness of stars and other objects in the sky using a system called "apparent magnitude." The idea began when ancient stargazers divided the stars into six ranks, from the brightest "stars of the first magnitude" to the faintest they could see with the naked eye in the sixth magnitude. Today, the system has been given a more scientific grounding using electronic measurements and has been extended to cover much brighter and much fainter objects.

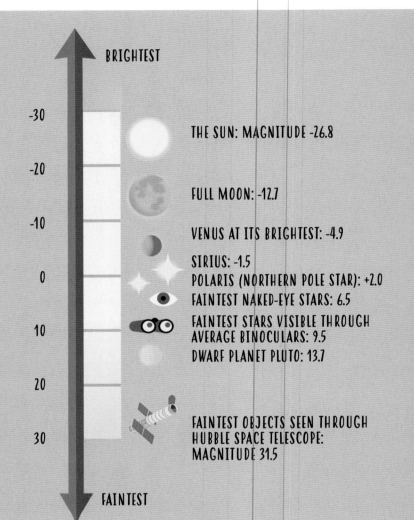

BRIGHTEST

-30
-20
-10
0
10
20
30

FAINTEST

THE SUN: MAGNITUDE -26.8

FULL MOON: -12.7

VENUS AT ITS BRIGHTEST: -4.9

SIRIUS: -1.5
POLARIS (NORTHERN POLE STAR): +2.0
FAINTEST NAKED-EYE STARS: 6.5
FAINTEST STARS VISIBLE THROUGH AVERAGE BINOCULARS: 9.5
DWARF PLANET PLUTO: 13.7

FAINTEST OBJECTS SEEN THROUGH HUBBLE SPACE TELESCOPE: MAGNITUDE 31.5

❓ OUT OF CURIOSITY

A star's apparent magnitude does not reflect its actual light output, known as its luminosity. A sixth-magnitude star could be highly luminous but very far away, while a brilliant first-magnitude star could be fairly average but very close to our solar system.
In order to measure a star's true luminosity, astronomers need to know both its apparent magnitude and its distance.

COLOR AND TEMPERATURE

Stars vary in color from red through orange and yellow to white, blue, and even violet. The precise color depends on the star's surface temperature. Like a metal bar being heated in a furnace, stars glow red-hot at relatively low temperatures, then yellow and white hot, before eventually glowing blue if they get hot enough. Red stars have temperatures as low as 3,000 °C (5,800 °F), while blue stars may be ten times as hot. Our Sun is a yellow star with a surface temperature of 5,500 °C (9,900 °F).

3,000 °C   6,000 °C   10,000 °C   30,000 °C

PARALLAX AND DISTANCE

The distance to a star is one of the most valuable pieces of information astronomers can find out, but how can you measure such a huge distance when it's impossible to travel there? The most direct method, called **parallax** measurement, makes use of the way a nearby star's direction in the sky appears to change from different points of view on Earth.

As Earth moves from one side of its orbit to the other over six months, we see stars from two points of view separated by 300 million km (186 million miles). This is a large enough separation for the direction of nearby stars to change by a tiny detectable amount. The size of its parallax reveals how far away the star is.

You can see the parallax effect for yourself simply by holding up a pencil at arm's length. Cover one eye and then the other, and you'll see that the pencil seems to shift direction because each eye has a separate point of view.

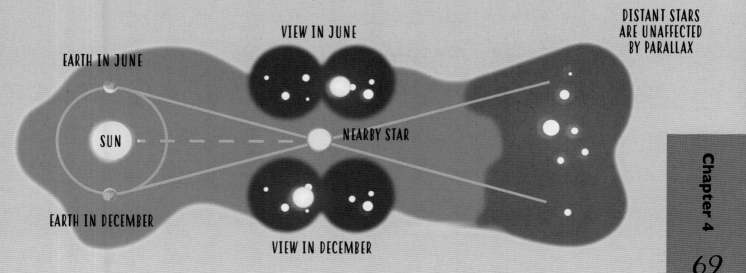

VIEW IN JUNE

DISTANT STARS ARE UNAFFECTED BY PARALLAX

EARTH IN JUNE

SUN

NEARBY STAR

EARTH IN DECEMBER

VIEW IN DECEMBER

SECRETS OF STARLIGHT

Stars give out light (and other types of electromagnetic radiation) with a range of energies and wavelengths. By measuring the radiation of different stars, astronomers can calculate their temperatures, what they are made of, and how they are moving.

SPECTROSCOPY

Visible light is made up of different colors of different wavelengths. These can be seen when light passes through a wedge-shaped glass called a prism and is split into its rainbow colors. The rainbowlike band of colors given off by a star is called its emission spectrum. It can reveal a lot about the nature of a star. The study of spectra is called spectroscopy.

The band of a star's spectrum varies in both color and intensity. A star produces its most light at a wavelength and color related to its surface temperature.

If the spectrum is spread out widely, dark **absorption lines** can be seen. This is where material between us and the light source (often gases in the star's atmosphere) is absorbing certain light energies. The energy levels absorbed are unique to each type of atom or molecule doing the absorbing, so astronomers can identify the chemicals involved.

OUT OF CURIOSITY

A star's apparent color depends on how our eyes interpret the mix of light that it emits—like paints mixed on a palette. The hottest stars emit lots of blue light but very little red. Because green lies in the middle of the spectrum, stars that emit the most green light tend to produce equal amounts of blue and red. The result is that the colors balance out to produce a white rather than a green star.

TWO TYPES OF SPECTRA

While stars produce a rainbowlike spectrum covering a wide range of wavelengths, other space objects, such as gas clouds, produce light by emitting energy in very narrow wavelength bands. The result is a spectrum that is largely black with a few bright lines called **emission lines**. Just like dark absorption lines, these can be used to identify the chemicals involved.

HOW IS IT MOVING?

Want to know how a star or other space object is moving? Just study its spectrum! If an object's absorption or emission lines seem to match up to a known element but are slightly out of place, then it's a sign that their source is moving toward or away from Earth.

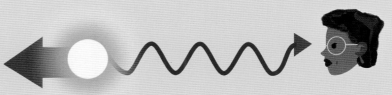

Light from sources moving toward Earth gets compressed into shorter wavelengths, or "blue shifted," while light from sources moving away from Earth is stretched into longer wavelengths, or "red shifted." Figure out the amount of red or blue shift, and you can discover the speed of the star's movement toward or away from Earth.

BINARIES, MULTIPLES, AND CLUSTERS

Many stars come in pairs, called binaries, or larger groupings, called multiples, with the stars orbiting each other under the influence of gravity. These binary and multiple stars are a result of the way that stars are born.

ORBITING TOGETHER

Unlike planets orbiting a star, stars in a binary (two part) or multiple (many part) system have roughly similar amounts of material (known as mass). Instead of one star staying still and others orbiting it, each star orbits a point in the middle, the "center of mass". Stars with lower mass orbit further away, while those with higher mass orbit more closely, rather like weights balancing on a seesaw.

A few binary and multiple stars can be seen using telescopes. Many others, however, are detected from their emissions spectrum (see page 70).

Depending on the separation between them, stars in a binary or multiple system may take anything from a few hours to millions of years to complete an orbit. By measuring their orbital speeds, astronomers can figure out each star's relative mass.

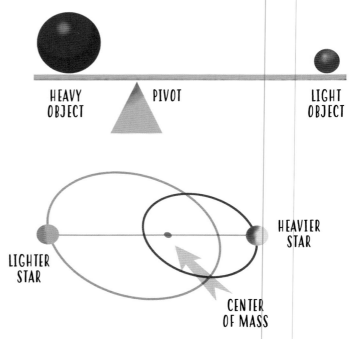

HEAVY OBJECT   PIVOT   LIGHT OBJECT

LIGHTER STAR   HEAVIER STAR   CENTER OF MASS

COSMIC LABORATORIES

Binaries and multiples formed from the same materials as each other have the same age and are the same distance from Earth. This means that astronomers can investigate any differences between the stars by looking at other factors, such as a star's mass.

FAMOUS MULTIPLES AND BINARIES

With a star map and binoculars or a small telescope, you can easily track down some of these amazing star systems for yourself.

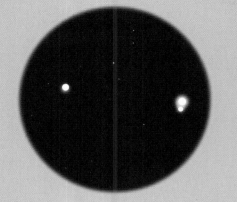

1) Mizar and Alcor

Mizar is the middle "star" in the tail of the constellation Ursa Major. You can spot its fainter companion Alcor, half a Moon's-width away, with your unaided eye. Astronomers aren't sure if Mizar and Alcor orbit each other, but if you zoom in on Mizar with a telescope, you'll see that this star is itself a binary system.

2) Albireo

Albireo marks the beak of Cygnus, the constellation of the Swan, which points south along the Milky Way. A small telescope will reveal it as a stunning double made up of a brighter orange star and a fainter blue companion.

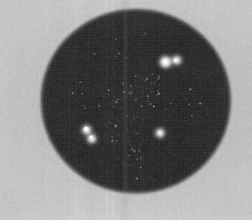

3) Epsilon Lyrae

Epsilon Lyrae in the constellation of the Lyre (an ancient musical instrument) is the sky's most famous multiple star, a "double double" that appears as a pair of stars to binoculars, but which turns out to be four stars through larger telescopes.

STAR CLUSTERS

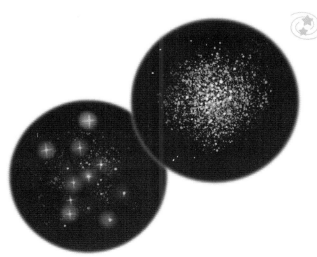

Alongside double and multiple systems, there are larger groups of stars known as star clusters. These are stars that formed together at the same time. The stars within loose "open clusters" have drifted apart over millions of years, but when the Milky Way galaxy was forming long ago, much bigger "globular clusters" were created. These had enough gravity to hold on to their members, so they have survived as dense balls of stars billions of years later.

PUTTING IT ALL TOGETHER

By comparing the temperature, luminosity, distance, and mass of different stars, as well as the spectra of their light, astronomers have identified hidden patterns and distinct types of stars.

✦ STARS OF ALL KINDS

The varying brightness and color of the stars you can see in the night sky is a reflection of both their properties and their distance from Earth. Visibility distance is how far a star can be seen across space. Luminosity is the star's actual light output. Different types of stars are given different names.

Blue supergiant
Visibility distance: Thousands of light years
Luminosity: 10,000 to 100,000 Suns
Temperature: Around 20,000 °C (36,000 °F)
Mass: 10 Suns or more

White star
Visibility distance: Hundreds of light years
Luminosity: Tens of Suns
Temperature: Around 10,000 °C (18,000 °F)
Mass: 1.4—2.1 Suns

Yellow star
Visibility distance: Tens of light years.
Luminosity: Close to that of the Sun.
Temperature: Around 5,500 °C (9,900 °F)
Mass: 0.7—1.3 Suns

Red dwarf
(Very faint red star.)
Visibility: Only seen through telescopes.
Luminosity: 1/100 to 1/100,000 of the Sun
Temperature: Around 3,000 °C (5,400 °F)
Mass: 0.1—0.6 Suns

Red giant
Visibility distance: Thousands of light years
Luminosity: Hundreds to thousands of Suns
Temperature: Around 3,000 °C (5,400 °F)
Mass: Similar to the Sun or greater

THE HERTZSPRUNG-RUSSELL DIAGRAM

Just over 100 years ago, astronomers Ejnar Hertzsprung and Henry Norris Russell had the idea of comparing the luminosities of stars with their temperatures on a graph, now called the Hertzsprung-Russell or H-R diagram. This revealed that the vast majority of stars follow a simple rule, and exceptions form distinct groups.

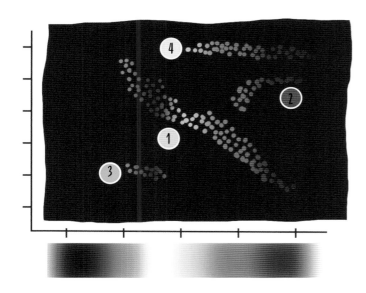

1 Nearly all stars lie on a diagonal band called the main sequence, where the brighter a star is, the hotter its surface. The main sequence links red dwarfs, through yellow stars like the Sun and white stars like Sirius, to the brightest blue stars. Brighter and hotter main-sequence stars are also more massive than fainter, cooler ones.

2 Red giants form a distinct group of bright but cool stars.

3 White dwarfs are stars much fainter than the Sun but with very hot surfaces.

4 A band of luminous supergiants runs across the top of the diagram. These are the most massive stars known.

READING THE H-R DIAGRAM

A star's position on the diagram depends on its energy output, size, and mass. The huge numbers of stars on the main sequence show that this is where the vast majority of stars spend most of their lives. A star's mass determines just where it sits on the diagonal band. Most stars keep the same mass for most of their lives, so they stay in the same spot throughout their "main sequence lifetime."

When a star nears the end of its life, it can move out of the main sequence.
• Red giants are stars that have brightened and increased in size, turning redder. They can be various masses.
• White dwarfs are the last stage in the life of Sun-like stars. There are plenty of them, but their faintness makes them hard to see.
• Supergiants are stars with higher masses than normal. They are much rarer than normal stars.

WHERE STARS ARE BORN

Glowing clouds of gas and dust called emission nebulae are some of the most beautiful sights in the night sky. These are where stars are born, and go through their turbulent early years.

STAR BIRTH NEBULAE

Nebulae are large clouds of gas and dust floating in space. They may be hundreds of light years across. Some nebulae block light from objects behind them. Some reflect light. An **emission nebula** is a type that radiates its own light. Stars are born in nebulae when something pushes or pulls the gas together, and some clumps become dense enough to start pulling in more material from their surroundings. These "protostars" rapidly grow in size and get hotter and denser in the middle, until they start to shine.

TRIGGERS OF STAR FORMATION

What could push or pull a nebula's gas to trigger star formation? Astronomers believe there are three main causes:
- **Moving into a crowded region of the Milky Way called a spiral arm**
- **Other stars drifting past and pulling material towards them**
- **Shock waves from exploding giant stars pressing material together**

FAMOUS STAR BIRTH NEBULAE

Nebulae that are forming new stars glow because their gas is energized by powerful radiation from hot newborn stars. Winds of material blown from these stars shape their surroundings, while dust-filled areas form pillars, canyons, and blobs that appear dark against the glowing background. Here are some great nebulae to track down online or in the night sky:

Orion Nebula: Marking the sword of the constellation of Orion, the brightest nebula in the sky has a flower shape with four bright newborn stars in the middle.

Carina Nebula: This bright nebula, in the southern constellation of Carina the Keel, contains two young star clusters of different ages.

Eagle Nebula: This famous nebula, in the constellation of Serpens the Snake, is home to the "Pillars of Creation" (above), dark columns of gas and dust with stars forming inside them.

YOUNG STARS

Polar jets

As a knot of gas collapses to form a star, it spins faster and faster. Leftover dust and gas from the star's formation flattens into a disk around the star, but some is thrown into space from the star's poles, creating narrow jets that billow out into huge clouds farther from the star.

Unstable youth

Young stars can vary in brightness as they gain material, but eventually they settle down as they get hotter and brighter. Material orbiting the star may become the building blocks of a new solar system, featuring planets and moons.

DRIFTING APART

A single nebula can give rise to a cluster of hundreds or thousands of stars. Over millions of years, most of these stars will drift away, but astronomers can often trace these moving groups of stars back to their origin.

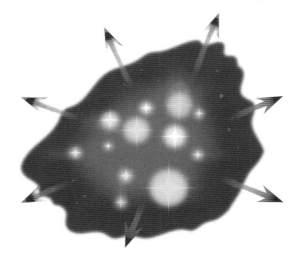

THE POWER SOURCE OF STARS

Just like the Sun, all stars shine through a process called nuclear fusion. This can happen in various ways, and the amount of power it generates determines not just a star's luminosity, size, and surface temperature, but also how long it may live for.

⭐ WHAT IS FUSION?

An atomic nucleus is the central part of all atoms, the tiny particles that make up all visible matter. Normally, the nucleus is orbited by even smaller particles called electrons, but deep inside a star, the temperature and pressure is so great that the electrons are stripped away and the nucleus is exposed. The nuclei of lightweight elements can then be forced together (fused) to create heavier ones.

⭐ THE P-P CHAIN

The most common type of fusion reaction used by stars is called the p-p (proton-proton) chain. This involves fusing nuclei of the lightest element, hydrogen, to make the next lightest element, helium. A hydrogen nucleus normally has just one "subatomic particle" called a proton, while a helium nucleus has four (two protons and two neutrons). It takes several steps to turn hydrogen into helium.

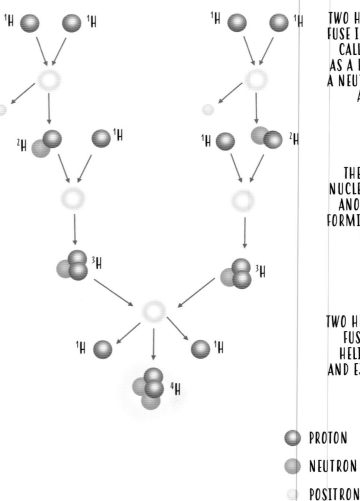

TWO HYDROGEN NUCLEI FUSE INTO A NEW FORM CALLED DEUTERIUM. AS A PROTON BECOMES A NEUTRON IT RELEASES A POSITRON.

THE DEUTERIUM NUCLEUS FUSES WITH ANOTHER PROTON, FORMING A HELIUM-3 NUCLEUS.

TWO HELIUM-3 NUCLEI FUSE TO FORM A HELIUM NUCLEUS AND EJECT TWO SPARE PROTONS.

- 🔵 PROTON
- 🔵 NEUTRON
- ⚪ POSITRON

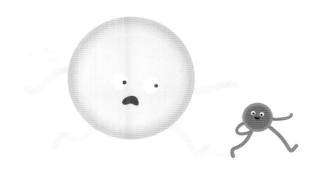

FAST OR SLOW?

Because it involves so many stages, the p-p chain reaction releases energy at a slow rate, allowing stars that rely on it to shine for billions of years. The greater a star's mass, the hotter and denser its core and the faster this reaction runs.

Stars with a higher mass than the Sun, however, can turn hydrogen to helium using a different process called the **CNO cycle**. This involves protons fusing with heavier carbon nuclei in the star's core, turning them into nitrogen and oxygen before releasing helium and carbon that can be used again.

The CNO cycle turns hydrogen to helium much more quickly than the p-p chain, so stars heavier than the Sun can shine far more brightly, but also use up their hydrogen fuel more quickly. Because of this, a massive star may run out of fuel in just a few million years, while a low-mass faint star can keep shining for thousands of times longer.

OUT OF CURIOSITY

Each stage in the fusion process generates energy. This is because the particles made or released by the process weigh slightly less than the ones which go into it. The excess mass is converted into energy.

BALANCING ACT

Every star is caught in a balancing act between the inward pull of gravity on its outer surface, and the outward push of hot matter and radiation trying to escape from inside. Both gravity and the rate of energy generation depend on the star's mass. Together they determine the size of the star, its temperature, and color. If nothing else changes, a larger surface provides more room for energy to escape, so the surface is heated less and is cooler than if the star was smaller.

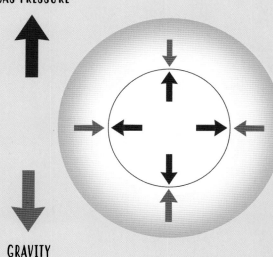

GAS PRESSURE

GRAVITY

OTHER PLANETARY SYSTEMS

The first exoplanets (planets orbiting other stars) were discovered in 1992. Astronomers have now tracked down more than 5,000 of them. There could be as many planets as stars in the Milky Way.

DISCOVERING EXOPLANETS

Planets around other stars are almost impossible to see directly. They're far too faint and are easily drowned out by the glare of their stars. For this reason, astronomers have to use clever tricks to identify **exoplanets** and measure their properties. Two methods that work well are the radial-velocity method and the transit method.

LIGHT IS BLUE SHIFTED WHEN STAR MOVES TOWARD EARTH.

STAR'S ORBIT IS AFFECTED BY A HIDDEN PLANET.

LIGHT IS RED SHIFTED WHEN STAR MOVES AWAY FROM EARTH.

RADIAL VELOCITY

Planets that are heavy or close to their stars tug on them as they orbit, causing the star to wobble slightly. Astronomers can detect their radial motion (movement toward or away from Earth) by measuring the blue and red shift in the star's spectrum (page 70). This gives them an idea of the planet's mass, as well as its orbital period (year) and distance from its star.

TRANSIT METHOD

If a planet's orbit happens to line up with the direction of Earth, then it will sometimes pass in front of its star. This event is called a **transit**. It causes the star's brightness to dip by a tiny amount since part of its surface is blocked from view. Transits are easier to spot (and more likely to happen) when a planet is in a close orbit.

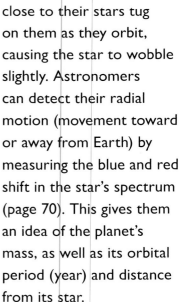

1   2   3

KEPLER

More than half the known exoplanets were discovered by Kepler, a space telescope that operated from 2009 to 2018. Kepler's mission involved staring at a single small patch of sky, measuring the brightness of 150,000 individual stars continuously for more than three years to spot transits.

PLANETS OF ALL KINDS

The discovery of exoplanets has shown that planets can be much more varied than those in our own solar system. These strange new worlds include:

Gas planet cores: Large rocky worlds close to their stars. They are thought to be hot gas giants that have lost their outer layers of gas.

Mini-Neptunes: Planets that are gas giants but have only about half the mass of Neptune.

Water worlds: Planets with the right conditions for deep oceans to cover their surface (though water has yet to be confirmed).

Super-Earths: Worlds that are thought to be mostly rocky, but have a mass up to ten times that of Earth.

Hot Jupiters: Gas giant planets that orbit very close to their stars and have atmospheres inflated by the heat.

GOLDILOCKS ZONES

Astronomers can calculate the temperature of an exoplanet based on the properties of its parent star and the size of its orbit. At the right distance from a star, known as the Goldilocks zone, temperature conditions may be right for liquid water on the surface, and possibly even alien life.

CHANGING STARS

Not all of the stars in the sky shine steadily. Many brighten or dim from time to time. In some stars, changes in brightness occur regularly, while in others the change is unpredictable. Binary stars don't actually change their brightness, but the path of their orbits mean they appear to dim at times.

PULSATING STARS

Stars can pulsate (change their luminosity) at various times in their lives. This is usually due to changes in their internal structure. As the star expands and cools, pressure drops until gravity takes over and pulls the star inward. As it contracts and heats up, the star brightens until pressure from within pushes it outward once again. Pulsating stars can vary in brightness over hours or many months.

ECLIPSING BINARIES

Some **variable stars** are actually binary systems, a pair of stars whose orbits line up so that they pass in front of each other as seen from Earth. As each star blocks part of the other's light, their combined brightness dips.

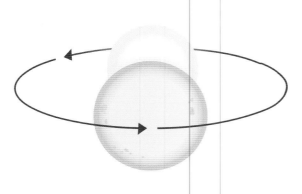

FAMOUS VARIABLES

Delta Cephei
A bright yellow supergiant in the constellation of Cepheus that pulsates in a 5.4-day cycle.

Mira
A pulsating red giant in the constellation of Cetus that varies in brightness over 332 days, from being a fourth-magnitude naked-eye star, to being visible only with a telescope.

Algol
An eclipsing binary in the constellation of Perseus that dips from second to third magnitude during 10-hour-long eclipses every 69 hours.

IMPOSTER ERUPTIONS

The most massive stars are doomed to end their lives in **supernova** explosions, but before they die they become increasingly unstable. This leads to outbursts called supernova imposters, where the star brightens enormously and throws out a huge cloud of gas, before fading and recovering.

In the 1830s, a distant star named Eta Carinae erupted to become the second-brightest star in the entire sky. It's on its way to becoming a supernova.

NOVA SYSTEMS

Another type of eruption is called a **nova** (Latin for "new star"). These happen in binary star systems where a white dwarf orbits close enough to its companion for its gravity to pull gas away from the other star. The white dwarf builds up layers of gas on its hot surface, which then ignites in a sudden burst of fusion, causing the system to brighten for weeks or months.

SOOTY STARS

Some stars are prone to sudden dips, rather than increases, in their brightness. Some red giants, for example, can create huge clouds of dust at cool spots in their atmosphere. If these are blown out into space, they can block light reaching Earth, even though the star's overall brightness may not have changed.

From 2019 to 2020, the bright red star Betelgeuse in Orion dimmed to two-thirds of its normal brightness when a vast cloud of soot blocked its light. As the dust cleared, astronomers were able to see the star at full brightness again.

HOW STARS DIE

Stars spend most of their lives fusing hydrogen to helium in their cores. Once that fuel supply runs out, the star goes through major changes as it heads towards the end of its life.

✳ RED GIANTS AND PLANETARY NEBULAE

As the energy coming from a star's core grows weaker, the layers above it start to fall inward. This makes them hotter and denser and means that fusion can begin around the core. The increased heat makes the fusion run much faster, so the star glows brighter. Above the fusion layer, the star then expands and its surface cools, so it becomes a **red giant**.

Stars like the Sun can bounce back from their first red giant phase, restarting fusion in their cores, which now turns helium into heavier elements such as carbon. Eventually, the helium in the core runs out, and the star swells once again.

The dying red giant pulsates and creates powerful stellar winds that cast its outer atmosphere outwards to form a cosmic smoke ring called a **planetary nebula**. The nebula glows as it is energized by light from the star's exposed super-hot core.

OUT OF CURIOSITY

Planetary nebulae have nothing to do with planets. The name comes from the first ones discovered in the late 1700s. Several astronomers compared their glowing rings to ghostly planetlike disks.

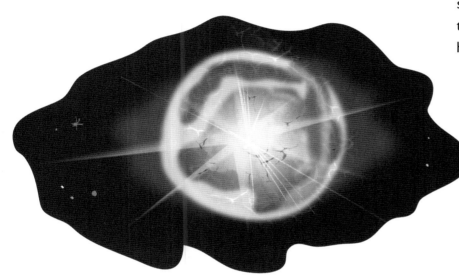

SUPERGIANTS AND SUPERNOVAE

As their lives come to an end, the most massive stars of all, the supergiants, can fuse elements heavier than helium and develop a series of layers, or shells, around their core. Eventually, the star tries to fuse iron nuclei, a step which uses energy rather than generates it. With its energy source lost, the star's balancing act ends, and the core collapses with such force that a shockwave rebounds through the upper layers, tearing the star apart in a huge supernova explosion.

A supernova shockwave produces so much heat and pressure that many rare forms of fusion become possible, with nuclei fusing to form every possible natural element. The energy released by the exploding star can outshine an entire galaxy.

SUPERNOVA REMNANTS

As the explosion of a supernova fades, it leaves behind a rapidly expanding gas cloud called a supernova remnant. Gas inside the cloud may be heated to millions of degrees and emit powerful X-rays as well as visible light. Astronomers can track the expansion of supernova remnants from year to year, as they spread a rich mix of elements made in the supernova across nearby space.

The Crab Nebula in the constellation of Taurus is the remnant of a supernova that was seen by Chinese astronomers in 1054.

WHAT STARS LEAVE BEHIND

Most stars that die leave behind either a white dwarf or a neutron star.
These pack much of the original core's mass into a much smaller space.
The most massive stars of all produce an even stranger object—a black hole.

WHITE DWARFS

A **white dwarf** is left behind when a star with less than eight times the Sun's mass sheds its outer layers in a planetary nebula. This leaves the star's hot inner core exposed, but because nuclear reactions can no longer support it from inside, the core collapses under is own weight until it's roughly the same size as Earth. The result is a slowly cooling dead star so densely packed that a teaspoonful of its material would weigh as much as a full-grown elephant.

SIRIUS B

The most famous white dwarf is Sirius B, the faint companion of the brightest star in the sky. Sirius B is all that remains of a star that was once larger and brighter than the main star we know as Sirius A, but raced through its life cycle to leave a white dwarf behind.

NEUTRON STARS AND PULSARS

When a massive star dies in a supernova explosion, its core collapses so violently that it leaves behind fast-spinning remains called a **neutron star,** which is even denser than a white dwarf. A neutron star packs about 1.4 times the mass of the Sun into a city-sized ball.

As a star's core collapses, it concentrates the original star's magnetism, creating a powerful magnetic field that forces out jets of radiation from the poles.

Because the magnetic poles don't usually line up precisely with the star's rotation, the jets sweep around the sky as the neutron star spins. From a distance, the result is a **pulsar**, a rapidly blinking source of radio waves, light, and other radiations.

LITTLE GREEN MEN?

When astronomers Jocelyn Bell and Anthony Hewish discovered the first pulsar in 1967, they were so puzzled by its regular radio signal that they briefly wondered if it might be a beacon set up by aliens. For a time, the pulsar was even known by the codename LGM-1, short for "Little Green Man."

BLACK HOLES

If the collapsing core of a supernova is heavy enough, then a massive star can leave behind the strangest stellar remains of all, a **black hole**.

Black holes concentrate all the mass of the star's core into a single tiny point called a **singularity**.

The singularity's gravity is so strong that it pulls in anything that gets too close. Within a certain distance, even light, the fastest thing in the Universe, cannot escape from its gravity, so the singularity is surrounded by a wall of darkness called the **event horizon**, the outside surface of the black hole.

RELATIVISTIC JETS.
RADIATION AND PARTICLES
EMITTED BY THE BLACK HOLE.

EVENT HORIZON.
LIGHT AND MATTER
CANNOT ESCAPE BEYOND
THIS POINT.

ACCRETION DISC.
THIS SPINNING MATTER
WILL BE PULLED INTO
THE BLACK HOLE OR
EJECTED INTO SPACE.

OUT OF CURIOSITY

A black hole itself doesn't emit light or other radiation, but it can be detected in other ways. If one star in a binary system becomes a black hole, then the other star's orbit will reveal the mass of its unseen companion. If material from nearby space is falling into the black hole, there are other signs. The material forms a disk that gets hotter towards the middle and emits powerful forms of radiation before it reaches the event horizon. Black holes also have powerful magnetic fields that can fling out some of the shredded material from this disk in high-speed jets.

CHAPTER 5

THE MILKY WAY AND BEYOND

The Milky Way is our home galaxy, a vast spiral of stars, planets, gas, and dust held together by its own gravity. Every star we can see in the night sky is part of this system, but the Milky Way is just one of countless galaxies in the wider Universe.

In this chapter, we'll find out how our galaxy is mapped and look at what's hiding in its heart. We'll also examine different kinds of galaxies and discover why scientists think a huge part of the Universe is missing!

OUR GALAXY

The Milky Way gets its name from a band of light that runs across the night sky. It was only when astronomers like Galileo looked at it through telescopes in the early 1600s that they discovered it was made up of countless faint stars.

🌀 THE PATH OF THE MILKY WAY

The Milky Way follows a path across the night sky with its northernmost point in the constellation (group of stars) of Cassiopeia and its southernmost point in the constellation of Crux. It is at its broadest and brightest in the direction of the constellation of Sagittarius the Archer. Dark patches in the Milky Way are where clouds of dust block the light from more distant stars.

Either side of the Milky Way, the stars are more scattered against the blackness of empty space. This allows us to see across millions of light years, and spot other distant galaxies.

⑥ PLANE OF THE GALAXY

LOOKING OUT OF THE MILKY WAY

LOOKING ACROSS THE MILKY WAY

The Milky Way looks like a band of stars to us because the galaxy as a whole is a thick disk with our solar system inside. When we look across this disk, we see countless stars behind each other at a wide variety of distances. When we look out of it, however, we only see past the stars that are above and below the Sun in our part of the disk, with deep space lying beyond.

⑥ THE HERSCHELS' MAP

In the 1780s, astronomers William and Caroline Herschel made the first attempt to map the shape of the Milky Way (below). They assumed that stars were spread evenly through space, and counted the number they could see through a telescope in every direction. One problem with their theory was that they believed the Sun must lie in the middle of the Milky Way, rather than being much nearer its edge.

THE HERSCHELS' MAP OF THE MILKY WAY

THE SUN

? OUT OF CURIOSITY

The name "Milky Way" comes from Greek legend. The Greeks invented many of today's constellations and named them after gods, humans, and animals from their myths. In this case, they saw the pale stream of light as milk spilled by Hera, the queen of the gods. The word galaxy comes from the Milky Way's name in Latin, the *Via Lactea*.

It's hard to imagine the shape of the Milky Way when we are inside it looking out. Nearby stars, gas, and dust block our view of more distant parts of the galaxy. So, how did astronomers figure out its structure?

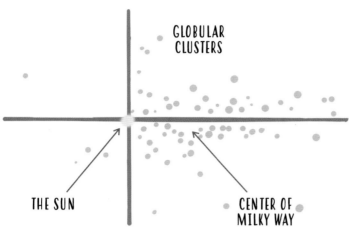

GLOBULAR
CLUSTERS

THE SUN

CENTER OF
MILKY WAY

FINDING OUR PLACE

Most stars, star clusters and nebulae lie in the flat disk of the Milky Way, but globular clusters (densely packed balls of stars) are often found above and below it, as marked on the chart (left). When astronomer Harlow Shapley mapped their positions and movements in the early twentieth century, he found they were not evenly spread around the sky. Instead, they move around a point 26,000 light years away in the direction of the constellation Sagittarius, the true center of the galaxy.

INTERSTELLAR CLOUDS

In the 1940s, Dutch astronomer Jan Oort realized that radio waves from hydrogen gas floating between the stars can pass straight through clouds of stars and dust. Using radio telescopes to map the Milky Way (right), he identified a pattern of hydrogen clouds that confirmed the galaxy's spiral structure.

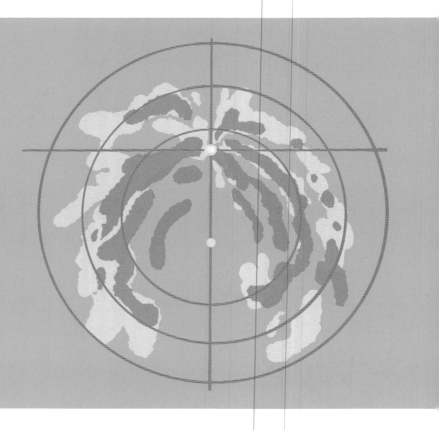

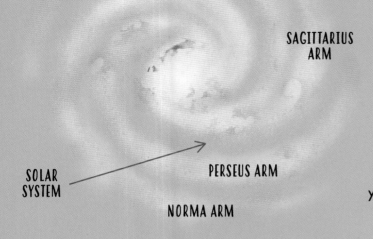

CENTAURUS ARM

SAGITTARIUS
ARM

SOLAR
SYSTEM

PERSEUS ARM

NORMA ARM

SPIRAL SHAPED

The latest measurements and observations reveal the Milky Way as a huge spiral galaxy, with two major spiral arms (and two minor ones) packed with newborn stars, clusters, and nebulae. The galaxy's "arms" emerge from the ends of a long bar of older red and yellow stars that cross the galaxy's central bulge. The visible stars are gathered closely in a disk about 120,000 light years across.

Our solar system lies roughly halfway between the middle and the edge of the Milky Way and takes about 230 million years to make one complete orbit around the center.

CENTRAL BULGE OF
THE MILKY WAY

WARPED SECTION

WARPED SECTION

EDGE-ON MILKY WAY

Seen from the side, our galaxy is a disk about 1,000 light years in thickness, with a central bulge roughly 10,000 light years wide. The disk is not flat. It twists down on one side and up on the other. Astronomers think this is due to another, smaller galaxy slowly passing through the Milky Way.

JUST THE FACTS

- The starry disk of the Milky Way is about 120,000 light years across.

- The plane of the galaxy is 1,000 light years deep, bulging to about 10,000 light years in the middle.

- The Milky Way contains 100 to 400 billion stars.

- It is thought to be about 13 billion years old.

Spiral galaxies like the Milky Way are cosmic whirlpools of gas, dust, and stars. But how do they form and keep their shape as they slowly rotate over billions of years?

⊚ WHY DON'T SPIRALS WIND UP?

We would expect the spinning motion of a galaxy's spiral arms to make them stretch and tighten around the center of a galaxy over time (as shown below). However, astronomers have never seen any examples of galaxies like this. This suggests that spiral arms are not permanent features but are continually re-forming themselves.

HOW A SPIRAL GALAXY MIGHT BE EXPECTED TO CHANGE OVER TIME ... BUT DOESN'T!

⊚ COSMIC RECYCLING

When old stars die, many of the elements created by nuclear fusion through their lifetimes are scattered across space. These heavier and more complex elements form a small but important part of the nebulae that produce later generations of stars, allowing them to make heavier elements still. In this way, spiral galaxies act like giant factories for the production of heavier elements.

⊚ INSIDE A SPIRAL ARM

Stars, gas, and dust move in and out of the spiral arms of galaxies. Passing through is like getting caught in a traffic jam—objects slow down and bunch together on their way through.

The spiral arm doesn't just push stars closer together. It also triggers the birth of new ones by compressing passing gas clouds into star-forming nebulae. Heavyweight stars born inside these nebulae are the brightest stars in the entire galaxy, but they only shine for a few million years. They use up their fuel relatively quickly before destroying themselves, but they help to light up the galaxy.

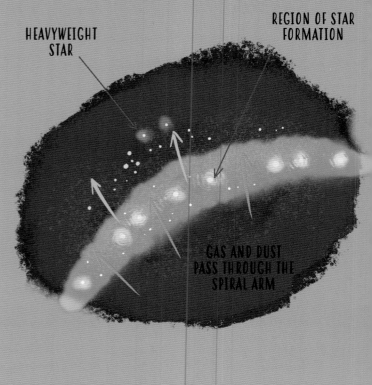

HEAVYWEIGHT STAR

REGION OF STAR FORMATION

GAS AND DUST PASS THROUGH THE SPIRAL ARM

ELEMENT ORIGINS

The Big Bang that created the Universe produced only the lightest elements—hydrogen, helium, and the lightweight metals lithium and beryllium.

The explosion of heavyweight stars in a supernova enrich the galaxy with heavy elements, such as tin, lead, and uranium.

THE BIG BANG

SUPERNOVA EXPLOSION

PLANETARY NEBULA

Planetary nebulae, which are created by the death of Sun-like stars, are rich in carbon, nitrogen, and oxygen.

STELLAR POPULATIONS

As the mix of elements it contains has changed, the Milky Way has produced two different types of stars that are found in different parts of the galaxy: early Population II and later Population I.

Population II: These cool red stars formed early in the galaxy's history. Made of almost pure hydrogen and helium, they shine slowly and steadily and have very long lifetimes. They are found today in the galaxy's central bulge and in clusters that orbit the Milky Way.

Population I: Stars in the galaxy's disk and spiral arms contain heavier elements than Population II, which allow them to use the CNO cycle of nuclear fusion (see page 79). This means that they shine brighter but burn through their fuel quickly and have shorter lifetimes.

THE HEART OF THE GALAXY

In the middle of the Milky Way's disk lies a vast bulge dominated by old red and yellow stars. These orbit a giant black hole that marks the true heart of our galaxy.

SPOTTING THE MIDDLE

The center of the Milky Way lies about 26,000 light years from Earth in the zodiac constellation of Sagittarius the Archer. This part of the sky is best seen on August and September evenings in the nborthern hemisphere—look for the brightest, thickest band of the Milky Way between Sagittarius and nearby Scorpius.

Spot the teapot-shaped pattern made by Sagittarius's bright stars. The middle of the galaxy lies close to the spout. This region of the sky is crowded with stars, clusters, and nebulae that are mostly in a spiral arm about 5,000 light years from Earth.

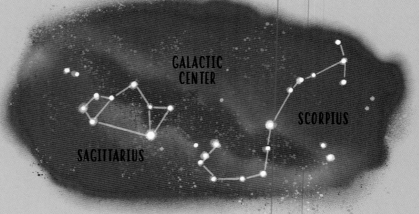

GALACTIC CENTER

SCORPIUS

SAGITTARIUS

FAST-MOVING STARS

Clouds of dust block starlight from the middle of the galaxy, but astronomers can use infrared satellites, radio telescopes, and radiation detectors to see what's going on there. These reveal a crowded section with 10 million stars packed into a region just three light years across. Most of these are old red stars, but there are also some bright young stars that formed just a few million years ago. Many of these young stars orbit at incredible speeds around something very small, very heavy, and completely invisible.

SUPERMASSIVE BLACK HOLE

The heart of our galaxy is a black hole much larger than those formed by the deaths of individual stars. The orbits of stars that pass close by show that it weighs about the same as four million Suns. Most of the space close to the black hole is empty, but small amounts of gas falling into the black hole emit radio waves before they disappear completely.

EVENT HORIZON TELESCOPE

In 2022, radio astronomers created the first image of the Milky Way's central black hole. By linking radio telescopes around the world in a network called the Event Horizon Telescope, they were able to see a doughnut-shaped ring of radio emission from the central region. The hole in the middle is the silhouette of the black hole itself.

THE GALAXY GALLERY

Galaxies come in many shapes and sizes, from spirals like
the Milky Way to clumps of gas where stars are born, and balls
of ancient red and yellow stars.

HUBBLE'S CLASSIFICATION

Edwin Hubble, the astronomer who first confirmed the existence of other
galaxies beyond the Milky Way, identified four different types:

- **Elliptical galaxies are compact balls of red and yellow stars that vary
  in shape from perfect spheres to stretched oval shapes.**

- **Spirals have a hub of red and yellow stars surrounded
  by a flattened disk of stars, gas, and dust.**

- **Barred spirals are similar
  to regular spirals except that
  the arms emerge from either
  side of a central bar shape.**

- **Lenticular galaxies are
  spirals with a central hub
  and disk full of gases, but not
  enough stars forming to
  shape spiral arms.**

SPIRALS

ELLIPTICAL GALAXIES

LENTICULAR
GALAXY

BARRED SPIRALS

IRREGULARS AND DWARFS

Today's astronomers recognize two other main types of galaxies:

- **Irregulars (right) are fairly shapeless, rich in gas,
  and have plenty of ongoing star formation.**

- **Dwarf spheroidals are small and dim galaxies
  with relatively few and older stars.**

THE LOCAL GROUP

The Milky Way and its nearest galaxies form a small cluster of galaxies called the Local Group. The group includes two other spirals: the large Andromeda Galaxy and the smaller Triangulum Galaxy. The Milky Way and Andromeda each have several smaller satellite galaxies in orbit around them. The combined gravity of both major spirals holds on to outlying galaxies in a region of space about 10 million light years across.

The Milky Way's biggest and brightest satellite galaxies are the Large and Small Magellanic Clouds, irregular galaxies best seen from Earth's southern hemisphere.

SPOTTING ANDROMEDA

The Andromeda Galaxy is the most distant thing you can see in the sky without a telescope. It is best seen in evening skies around November in the northern hemisphere. Look for the bright stars that form the square body of Pegasus the Flying Horse. The constellation of Andromeda is made up of two chains of stars joined to the northeast corner of the Square of Pegasus, south of the W-shaped constellation of Cassiopeia.

To spot the galaxy under dark skies, imagine a line bridging the third stars of each chain, then follow it a little way to the north. Binoculars or a small telescope will show it as a fuzzy patch of light wider than the full moon, with a brighter oval in the middle.

CASSIOPEIA

ANDROMEDA GALAXY

PEGASUS

ANDROMEDA

? OUT OF CURIOSITY

The constellation of Andromeda is named after a princess in Greek mythology, with links to several other nearby constellations. According to the story, Queen Cassiopeia (wife of King Cepheus of Ethiopia) angered the gods by bragging of her daughter Andromeda's beauty. They sent a sea monster (the constellation Cetus) to attack the land, and the King and Queen were advised to chain Andromeda to a rock as a sacrifice to save the kingdom. She was saved by the hero Perseus, who used the terrifying severed head of the Gorgon Medusa to turn Cetus to stone.

HOW GALAXIES EVOLVE

Not every galaxy obeys the usual rules. These surprising galaxies have proved important to understanding how galaxies grow and change.

GALAXY SMASH UPS

So-called peculiar galaxies often combine distorted shapes with brilliant bursts of star formation. Improving telescopic views and clever computer models have shown that they are a result of intergalactic collisions or close encounters.

When spiral galaxies get close to each other, gravity pulls on their spiral arms and causes them to unwind. At the same time, it can compress gas clouds inside each galaxy, triggering huge waves of star formation known as starbursts.

GLIMPSE OF THE FUTURE

Our own Milky Way and the Andromeda Galaxy are currently heading toward a collision about 4.5 billion years from now. The event will result in the birth of many new stars, but the space between individual stars makes it highly unlikely that many will collide with each other.

IT'S ALL ABOUT THE GAS

When spiral galaxies collide and merge, much of the gas they contain is either used up in a starburst or forced out of the merged galaxy. The result may be a lenticular galaxy that slowly builds new spiral arms. Repeated galaxy mergers result in elliptical shapes with ancient stars and no gas.

CANNIBAL GALAXIES

When smaller galaxies move too close to larger ones, the more massive galaxy's gravity tears the lighter galaxy apart and eventually absorbs the smaller galaxy's gas and stars into itself.

ACTIVE GALAXIES

Many galaxies far beyond the Milky Way show unusual activity around their central regions. These so-called active galaxies feature bright, rapidly changing sources of light and other radiation, and produce narrow jets of high-energy particles. They are thought to be a result of a central supermassive black hole.

Stars and gases are pulled into the black hole through a thin disk, where they are heated to searing temperatures and give off intense light and other radiations. Some of the material escapes in jets from above and below the black hole. The Active Galactic Nucleus (AGN) at the center of a galaxy may appear in different forms.

Possible AGNs at the center of a galaxy include:

Seyfert galaxy:
This looks like a regular spiral galaxy, but it is a class of AGN with high-energy jets that can be detected emerging from its disk.

Quasar: The most-powerful type of AGN, with high-velocity jets emerging from a central disk.

Radio galaxy: Jets from above and below this AGN can be detected as they hit other material and give off radio waves.

OUT OF CURIOSITY

Quasars, or quasi-stellar objects, are an extremely bright type of Active Galactic Nucleus (AGN) that far outshine their surrounding galaxy. The most powerful quasars can be thousands of times brighter than the Milky Way! Astronomers believe quasars can be caused by black hole feeding frenzies during collisions between galaxies in the distant Universe.

MAPPING THE UNIVERSE

Astronomers can use clever shortcuts to map the way galaxies are scattered across space on the largest cosmic scales. What's more, viewing the most distant galaxies can also offer a glimpse of earlier phases in the history of the Universe.

COSMIC TIME MACHINE

When you look out into space, you're also looking back in time. Light is the fastest thing in the Universe, moving at a staggering 300,000 km per second (186,000 miles per second), but distances in space are even bigger. While light from the Moon takes just over a second to reach Earth, light from distant galaxies that you see through your telescope may have set out millions of years ago. Astronomers call this effect "lookback time." The starlight you see may have left its source at the time of the first humans, the dinosaurs, or even the formation of our planet.

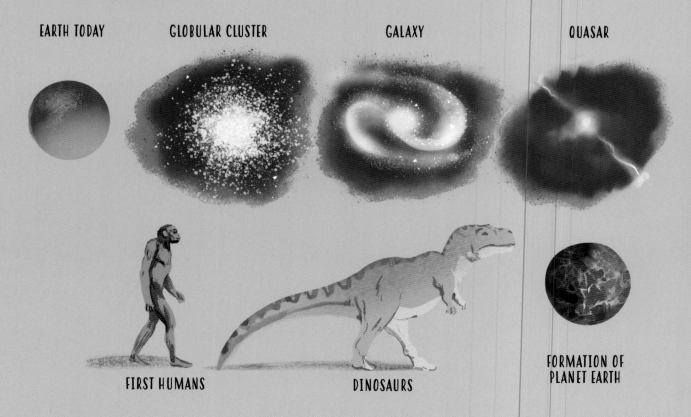

EARTH TODAY   GLOBULAR CLUSTER   GALAXY   QUASAR

FIRST HUMANS   DINOSAURS   FORMATION OF PLANET EARTH

Stars and galaxies change very slowly, so most nearby galaxies are more or less the same now as they were when their light set out to Earth. Over greater distances, however, lookback time makes a difference. The most powerful telescopes can pick up light from events billions of years ago, such as the violent collisions and galaxy mergers that powered quasars. Since such events are rare today, we don't see them in the nearby Universe, only at great distances.

MAPPING WITH REDSHIFT

Generally, the farther away a galaxy is, the faster it will be moving away from the Milky Way, and the more its light is stretched to the redder end of the color spectrum (see page 70). Astronomers can use this measure of **redshift** to estimate a galaxy's distance and create a map of the Universe.

REDSHIFT	LIGHT TRAVEL TIME
0.1	1.35 billion years
0.5	5.02 billion years
1.0	7.73 billion years
5.0	12.47 billion years
8.0	13.01 billion years
10.0	13.18 billion years

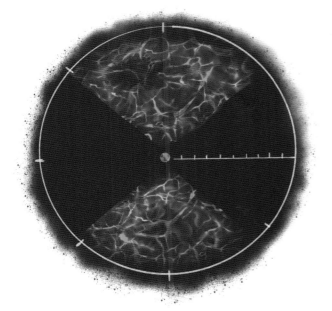

Projects such as the Sloan Digital Sky Survey use computer-controlled telescopes to collect data from millions of galaxies. The map (left) shows a slice of the sky to a redshift of 0.15 (about 2 billion light years). The dark areas show where light from distant galaxies is blocked by the Milky Way.

CLUSTERS, FILAMENTS, AND VOIDS

Most galaxies in the Universe are grouped in clusters, held together by their combined gravity. Our own Local Group (see page 99) is a fairly small example, but some clusters contain many hundreds of large galaxies. At an even larger scale, clusters are held together in superclusters. Large-scale maps of the Universe show that the superclusters form chains and sheets known as **filaments**. These filaments surround large, apparently empty areas called **voids**, like the film of soap around a bubble. Filaments and voids are the largest structures in the Universe.

THE DARK MATTER MYSTERY

Five-sixths of our Universe is missing! Individual galaxies and whole galaxy clusters behave as if they have far more gravity than can be accounted for by their visible matter. Astronomers believe an undetectable form of matter must be responsible.

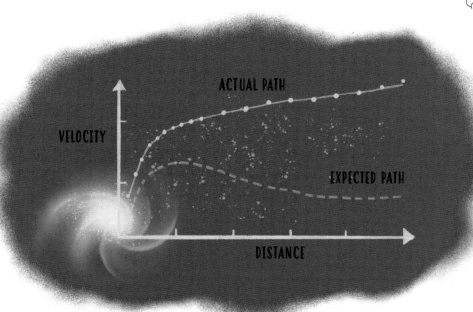

FIRST CLUE

In 1933, Swiss astronomer Fritz Zwicky measured the rate that galaxies spin at and found it far greater than expected. The galaxies behaved as if their cluster had much more mass and gravity than that he could observe. Zwicky blamed the problem on unseen material, which he called dark matter.

GALAXY ROTATION

In the 1970s, US astronomers Vera Rubin and Kent Ford set out to measure how spiral galaxies rotated. They used a spectroscope (see page 70) to detect how stars move at different distances from the central hub. They found that stars farther from the hub don't orbit more slowly, like planets around a star, but instead had roughly even speeds. The best explanation was that most of the galaxy's mass lay in a "dark matter halo" beyond the visible stars.

DETECTING DARK MATTER

Dark matter isn't simply dark. If it was, then it would still emit some form of electromagnetic radiation, or block light from other objects. Instead, it seems to be a completely unknown type of matter that is both dark and completely transparent. Light and other radiations pass straight through it. It can only be detected through the effects of its gravity.

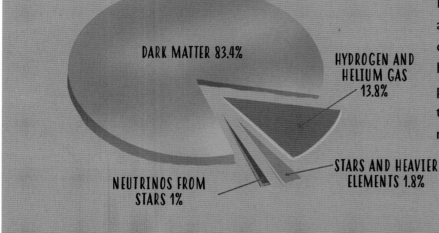

DARK MATTER 83.4%

HYDROGEN AND HELIUM GAS 13.8%

NEUTRINOS FROM STARS 1%

STARS AND HEAVIER ELEMENTS 1.8%

Radio telescopes and orbiting observatories allow astronomers to calculate how much of a contribution interstellar gas, dust made from heavier elements, and even tiny lightweight particles called neutrinos make to the mass of the Universe. Dark matter still weighs five times more than everything else put together.

SO WHAT IS IT?

Planets and black holes
Surveys of the Milky Way have ruled out the idea that objects made from normal matter, such as planets and black holes, could explain the extra mass. There simply aren't enough of them.

Fast-moving particles
Astronomers once hoped that hard-to-detect particles called neutrinos, which move at nearly the speed of light, might carry enough mass to solve the dark matter problem, but they turned out to be much too lightweight. What's more, dark matter seems to behave like slower-moving matter.

Something else
Scientists call the most likely form of dark matter Weakly Interacting Massive Particles (WIMPs for short). This means that dark matter is probably made up of small particles that can pass through other matter, and have enough mass to generate strong gravity when they cluster in large numbers.

CHAPTER 6

THE STORY OF THE UNIVERSE

Cosmology is the branch of astronomy that aims to discover the story of the entire Universe, from its mysterious beginnings to its eventual fate. It involves everything from the nature of space itself, to the possibilities for life elsewhere and even whether our Universe is one of many.

In this chapter, we'll look at different scientific theories on how the Universe was born and what it will eventually become.

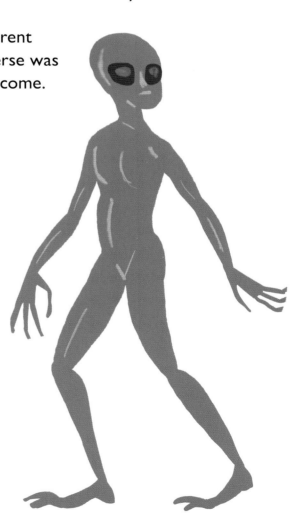

WHAT IS SPACE?

It's easy to think of space as just the empty gaps between stars and galaxies, but cosmologists see it differently. Space is the framework that sets the rules for how things move and behave.

SPACE IN 3D

We can rely on parallel lines remaining parallel however far we follow them, and we know there are three basic directions that an object can move—up and down, forward and backward, and left and right—each at right angles to the others. An easy way to think about space is as a 3D grid made up of cubes. But that's not always the case.

ENTER EINSTEIN

Albert Einstein was a talented German-born scientist who asked difficult questions about the nature of space. He wondered how the familiar laws of physics would apply to objects moving at close to the speed of light (the fastest thing in the Universe). In 1905, he explained how this would distort not only space around the object, but also the time it experienced. He called this the Special Theory of Relativity.

DISTORTED SPACE

In 1915, Einstein published his General Theory of Relativity. This explained that space and time are not only distorted by fast-moving objects, but also by objects with high masses. Space pinches in around massive objects a little bit like the neck of an hourglass or egg timer, while time runs more slowly. This is what causes the effect of gravity.

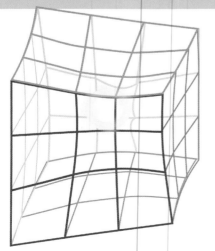

HOW A CUBIC AREA OF SPACE CAN BE DISTORTED BY AN OBJECT WITH A HIGH MASS.

COSMIC EXPANSION REVISITED

In the 1920s, Edwin Hubble proved that there were galaxies beyond our own. We now know that all galaxies are moving away from each other, and that the farther away a galaxy is, the faster it is likely to be moving away from Earth. Understanding the real nature of space helps explain this cosmic expansion.

OUT OF CURIOSITY

Clocks onboard orbiting satellites run around 40 millionths of a second faster each day than those on the ground. This is because they're less affected by Earth's gravity—distorting space and time.

Distant galaxies moving away from Earth aren't simply moving through space. They're being carried along as space itself expands. Imagine space as the surface of a galaxy-covered balloon. Some galaxies are close together, others farther apart. As the balloon inflates, the space between galaxies grows. Galaxies farthest apart appear to move apart more rapidly.

Light from distant galaxies is stretched out or redshifted, as it crosses vast distances to reach Earth. The space it moves through is expanding all the time, so the light's waves are stretched.

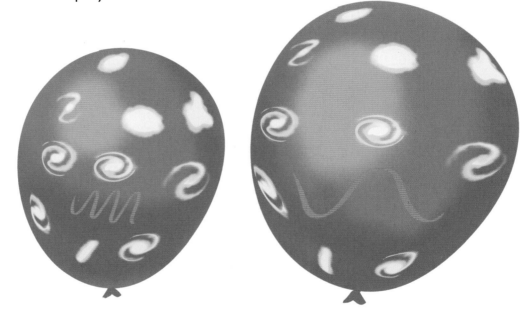

REWINDING EXPANSION

Until about 100 years ago, most astronomers believed that the Universe had been here forever, with no beginning or end. With the discovery that the cosmos is expanding, some scientists wondered what had happened at the beginning of the process. In 1931, Belgian priest and astronomer Georges Lemaître showed that this would mean that the very early Universe was much hotter because its matter was packed into a much smaller space. He called this point of origin the "primeval atom," but today we know it as the Big Bang.

HOW IT ALL BEGAN

The Big Bang was the moment when the Universe blinked into existence with an explosion about 13.8 billion years ago. That first instant remains mysterious, but the moments that followed saw the origin of the forces that control the Universe today.

THE BIG BANG

Although the Big Bang produced all the matter, or physical substances, in the Universe, from stars and galaxies to planets and dust clouds, its first moments were so extreme that matter as we currently know it could not exist. It was so hot that matter wasn't made of atoms or even smaller particles. Instead, it took the form of pure energy.

The Big Bang also marked the creation of space and time. One way to think of the Big Bang is as a bubble forming out of nowhere in a glass of soda, which began to rise and expand.

OUT OF CURIOSITY

The Big Bang created both space and time, so there was no time "before." Today, however, some cosmologists think that our Universe began with the moment of inflation (see opposite), perhaps popping out of a "multiverse" that launched many universes all the time.

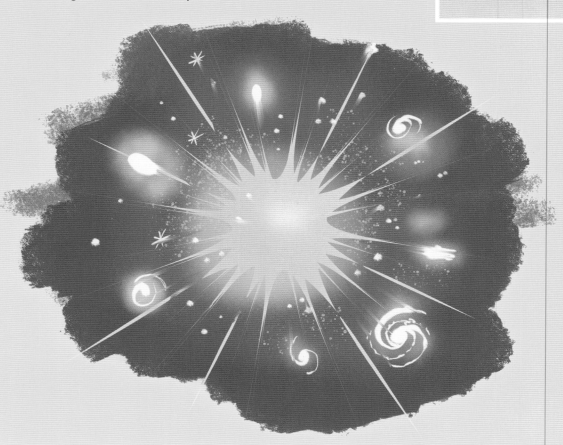

FORCES IN THE BIG BANG

In today's Universe, four separate forces control matter in different ways. Cosmologists think that during the Big Bang, these forces were combined, creating a single set of rules. As the Universe grew, temperatures dropped, and the forces separated, releasing huge amounts of energy.

ELECTROMAGNETISM: THE INTERACTION BETWEEN PARTICLES WITH ELECTRIC CHARGES.

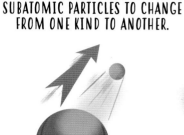

WEAK INTERACTION: ALLOWS SOME SUBATOMIC PARTICLES TO CHANGE FROM ONE KIND TO ANOTHER.

STRONG INTERACTION: HOLDS SUBATOMIC PARTICLES TOGETHER INSIDE THE ATOMIC NUCLEUS.

GRAVITY: INFLUENCES OBJECTS WITH MASS, AND IS STRONGER THE MORE MASS THAT IS PRESENT.

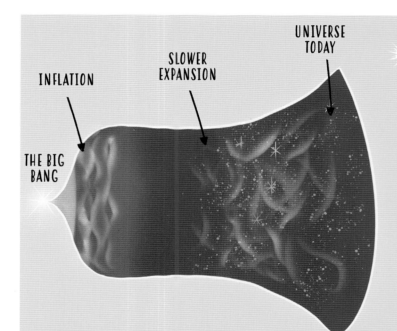

INFLATION

SLOWER EXPANSION

UNIVERSE TODAY

THE BIG BANG

INFLATION

A tiny fraction of a second after the Big Bang, energy released from the four main forces powered a sudden expansion of space, which blew up the newborn Universe to about one billion billion billion times its previous size.

After this brief moment, which scientists call "cosmic inflation," the Universe was still only the size of a basketball. It continued to expand at a slower rate. Tiny differences in this early Universe would swell to become the vast filaments and voids astronomers see today.

HOT STUFF

Temperatures during the Big Bang were unimaginably hot, but they fell rapidly as the Universe grew. At the earliest moment, cosmologists estimate the temperature was 100,000 billion billion billion degrees. By the end of cosmic inflation this had fallen to 1 billion billion billion degrees—and by the end of the first second, the temperature was "just" 10 billion degrees.

THE BIRTH OF MATTER

How did the vast amounts of energy in the Big Bang become everything we see in today's Universe? The answer involves the strange world of the very small, and the most famous equation in all of science.

EINSTEIN'S FAMOUS EQUATION

In 1905, Albert Einstein explored the mathematics of what would happen if an object moving at close to the speed of light (the fastest possible speed) was given a boost of energy. At slower speeds, this energy would normally cause the object to accelerate, but Einstein showed that, near light speed, it would cause the object's mass to increase. From this discovery, Einstein showed that energy (E) and mass (m) can be compared, according to the equation:

$$E = mc^2$$

where c^2 is the speed of light multiplied by itself.

Einstein's equation shows that small amounts of mass can be changed into large amounts of energy and therefore the Big Bang's energy could have been turned into subatomic particles.

MATTER AND ANTIMATTER

During the first fraction of a second, all the energy in the Universe was squeezed into a tiny space. Energy and mass were interchangeable, with particles constantly popping into existence.

These particles were created in pairs—matter and antimatter—each with an opposite electric charge. When matter and antimatter particles met, they destroyed each other and released their energy back into the Universe. For some reason, the Universe created slightly more matter than antimatter, so the particles we know today were able to survive.

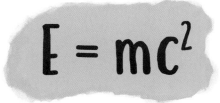

BUILDING THE ELEMENTS

As the Universe rapidly expanded, its energy became more spread out, and temperatures fell. This affected the energy available to produce particles, so the mass of new particles also fell rapidly.

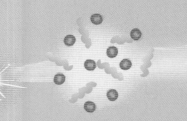
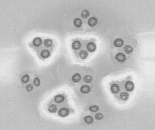
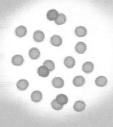

- **Quarks** were only produced for the first millionth of a second. Lighter particles called **leptons** could be made for the first ten seconds. The most common sort of lepton was electrons.

- Forces between quarks pulled them together to form larger particles—vast numbers of protons and a smaller number of neutrons.

- Within the first three minutes, the neutrons joined with protons and lightweight elements began to appear.

BACK TO THE BEGINNING

It's impossible for astronomers to look back and see the Big Bang, but modern technology can attempt to replicate some of it. Particle accelerators (such as the Large Hadron Collider in Switzerland) are enormous machines that launch streams of atomic nuclei at speeds close to that of light. When these nuclei collide and destroy each other, they release a burst of pure energy similar to that within the Big Bang. The energy is instantly converted back into particles with different masses. Scientific instruments measure these effects to better understand conditions in the early Universe.

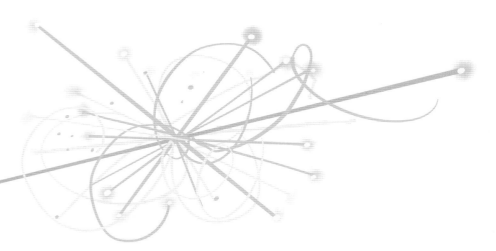

FIRST LIGHT

For the first 380,000 years of its history, the Universe was a foggy fireball. Then suddenly, as temperatures dropped, it became transparent. Amazingly, astronomers can detect light from this distant era and study it to find the secrets of the Big Bang.

FOGGY UNIVERSE

If you could travel back in time to the early Universe and withstand the heat, you'd see nothing but a steadily expanding fireball. The subatomic particles (electrons, neutrons, and protons) were so densely packed that light and other radiation could not travel far without bouncing off them in a new direction. With light unable to travel in straight lines, the Universe was hard to observe.

THE FOG CLEARS

About 380,000 years after the Big Bang, temperatures fell low enough (below about 2,700 °C or 4,800 °F) for electrons to combine with neutrons and protons for the first time. The first atoms were born, and the sudden reduction in free-floating particles allowed light to travel in straight lines at last.

ELECTRONS COMBINE WITH NEUTRONS AND PROTONS.

THE FIRST ATOMS.

A LONG JOURNEY

Radiation from the early fireball has been traveling in all directions ever since the beginning of the Universe. Astronomers can detect this radiation today. So, why doesn't the entire sky glow like a fireball? The reason lies in the expansion of the Universe (page 109). As the light has been traveling, space has been stretching, changing the light's wavelength, so that it is no longer visible or even infrared heat, but a weak radio signal that astronomers call the Cosmic Microwave Background Radiation (CMBR).

OUT OF CURIOSITY

Many scientists predicted the existence of the CMBR as a result of the Big Bang theory, but it was found by accident in 1964. Scientists Arno Penzias and Robert Woodrow Wilson were testing a new, sensitive radio antenna and found that whichever way they turned it, it still detected a weak signal. After investigating every possible cause of interference (including pigeon poop!) they were baffled—until a friend pointed out that the signal seemed to match predictions for the radiation left by the Big Bang.

MAPPING THE CMBR

Early measurements of the CMBR confirmed that it comes from all over the sky, but when satellites made more accurate maps in the 1990s and 2000s, they found tiny variations in the energy coming from different areas. These reveal spots that were slightly hotter or colder than average (by millionths of a degree) because the matter there was more densely or loosely packed. This pattern of denser and emptier regions is thought to have produced today's large-scale cosmic structure.

MAP SHOWING VARIATIONS IN THE COSMIC MICROWAVE BACKGROUND RADIATION.

LISTENING FOR WHISPERS

Between 2001 and 2010, a NASA satellite named the Wilkinson Microwave Anisotropy Probe (WMAP) charted the radiation in detail using a pair of small radio telescopes. WMAP's measurements allowed scientists to precisely date the age of the Universe to 13.772 billion years.

THE COSMIC WEB

How did the Universe go from a dense ball of subatomic particles to the web of galaxy clusters and superclusters mapped by today's astronomers? The answer may lie in the sudden inflation of the early Universe.

THE WEBLIKE STRUCTURE OF THE UNIVERSE

VOID

FILAMENTS, CONTAINING GALAXIES, GALAXY CLUSTERS, AND SUPERCLUSTERS

WHY DO GALAXIES CLUSTER?

Most of the visible matter in the Universe lies in galaxy clusters and superclusters, concentrated around large voids, or areas of empty space. How it got this way is still a mystery. Surveys of the Cosmic Microwave Background Radiation (see page 115) show tiny variations in the amount of matter, where gravity could act and pull in more material to form larger clumps. However, the amount of radiation bouncing around in the early foggy fireball should have stopped clumping from happening.

✾ DARK MATTER CLUES

Astronomers think the answer lies in **dark matter**, the unseen substance that makes up five-sixths of all mass in the Universe. Dark matter isn't just dark. It ignores light and other forms of radiation, so radiation couldn't stop it from forming clumps. When the Universe became transparent, matter was attracted to these clumps of dark matter.

✾ EXPLAINING STRUCTURE

The baby Universe contained very small ripples. When it expanded, the tiny ripples grew big enough to make a huge difference across the Universe.

But why can't we see these major variations from our viewpoint on Earth? Inflation helps provide an answer. Imagine an ant standing on an expanding balloon. When the balloon is small, the ant can see its curved edge and sense differences across the surface. As the balloon grows larger, the surface appears flatter and more uniform.

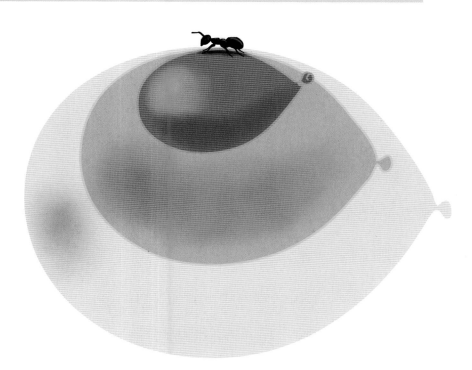

✾ LISTENING IN

Astronomers can't see back to before the Universe became transparent, but they may one day be able to track how dark matter came together in the ancient fireball. They hope to do this using **gravitational waves**. These are distortions in the shape of space (see page 108). Detecting gravitational waves would be like a doctor using a stethoscope to listen to a patient's body.

FIRST STARS AND GALAXIES

As the Universe became transparent and the fireball of the Big Bang faded, it was plunged into a cosmic dark age. Astronomers are now seeking the first stars and galaxies that brought light back to the darkness.

SEARCH FOR THE FIRST STARS

Over several hundred million years, in the cosmic dark ages, matter was drawn into clumps around dark matter. Within these clumps, the first stars began to form. Because they were made almost entirely of hydrogen and helium, they were able to grow much larger than any star can today.

NASA's James Webb Space Telescope, launched in 2021, is designed to search for this first generation of stars. Its 6.5 m (21.3 ft) segmented mirror and instruments are built to detect faint radiation that has been stretched to infrared wavelengths during its long journey across the Universe. The telescope carries a shade that protects it from the Sun's heat, so it can operate at temperatures below -223 °C (-370 °F).

GRAVITATIONAL LENSING

Astronomers can see distant galaxies if there is nothing blocking their light. To see galaxies hidden behind other objects, they use a clever trick called **gravitational lensing**. Because space is distorted by huge masses such as galaxy clusters (see page 116), rays of light passing close to them are pulled onto new paths. In this way, a massive object acts like a lens, bending and magnifying light from faint, distant objects such as the earliest stars and galaxies.

A CLUSTER IN THE WAY BENDS LIGHT

DISTANT GALAXY

EARLIEST GALAXIES

The death of the first stars produced enormous black holes, which sometimes collided and grew even more massive, pulling in material from their surroundings. Not all of this matter fell into the black holes. Collisions sometimes nudged it into safe, distant orbits and the matter became galaxies.

The first galaxies were shapeless clouds where new stars formed at a rapid rate. But as they collided, they formed more complex shapes, such as spirals.

LIFE IN THE UNIVERSE

Whether there's life elsewhere in the Universe is one of the biggest questions in science. Astrobiology is the branch of astronomy that tries to find answers, combining the discovery of exoplanets with new research into the origins of life on Earth.

WHAT IS LIFE?

There are many ways of defining life, but a simple one is that all living things, from tiny bacteria to complex plants and animals, find ways to extract energy and materials from their environment. They use these to grow, develop, and reproduce, while adapting to changes around them.

DNA

All life on Earth uses a complex chemical called DNA, which can store instructions telling living things how to grow and develop. Life on other worlds would need something like DNA to organize itself, grow, and reproduce. Knowing this helps astrobiologists look for the conditions needed for life to arise.

INGREDIENTS FOR LIFE

Life on Earth is the only example we have so far. It is sometimes described as carbon-based because DNA and other complex chemicals found in living things contain long chains of carbon atoms. Carbon would probably be crucial to alien life as well, because of the way its atoms can easily form bonds with other atoms. Carbon is widespread in the Universe—it's made inside stars and scattered across space when they die.

Another important requirement for life is a liquid environment where chemicals can move around, make contact, and go through chemical reactions. Water is the most likely liquid for the job, because it's widespread in the Universe, dissolves chemicals easily, and stays liquid over a wide temperature range.

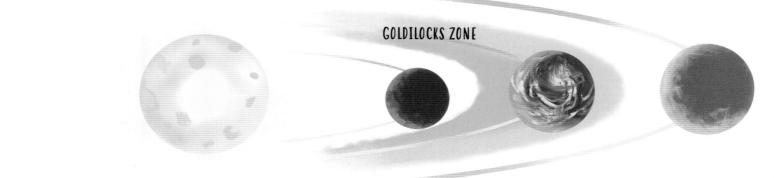

GOLDILOCKS ZONES

When looking for planets with the right ingredients for life, astrobiologists mostly look in a solar system's Goldilocks zone. This is the region where a planet is neither so hot that water boils away into space, nor so cold that it freezes completely. Instead, temperatures are just right for liquid water. Depending on the type of star the planet is orbiting, the Goldilocks zone may be farther out or much closer to the star than Earth's orbit around the Sun. Planets and moons in other parts of our solar system could also have liquid water buried underground.

BUILDING BLOCKS FROM SPACE

Astronomers have detected simple carbon-based chemicals in clouds between the stars, and more complex ones inside asteroids, comets, and meteorites. Many astrobiologists believe that these chemicals rained down on Earth early in its history, and that other worlds might have received similar "starter kits" for life.

OUT OF CURIOSITY

Life on other worlds would evolve to survive in its environment, and might have to solve the same challenges faced by life on Earth. Some planets might prevent life from evolving past simple single-celled organisms, but others could support more complex life—plants, animals, or things we can't even imagine. Fins, wings, and legs would be just as useful for swimming, flying, and walking life forms as they are on Earth, but there's no reason to think that the human shape is special. Humanoid aliens are extremely unlikely!

IS ANYBODY OUT THERE?

Even if life turns out to be widespread in our galaxy, there's no reason to think that minds would evolve on other planets in the same way. Despite this, the search for extraterrestrial intelligence continues.

RADIO SETI

Since the 1960s, astronomers have used radio telescopes to listen for messages from aliens. Although no definite signals have been detected, some mysterious bursts of radio waves are still unexplained decades after they were picked up.

Occasionally, SETI (Search for Extraterrestrial Intelligence) monitors stop listening and beam messages into the stars instead. The most famous of these was the "Arecibo message" beamed from a Puerto Rican telescope towards a distant globular star cluster in 1974.

FLYING SAUCERY?

Since the 1940s, there have been sightings of Unidentified Flying Objects (UFOs), which some people claim to have been alien spaceships or "flying saucers." However, with such huge distances between stars, aliens would be highly unlikely to waste time and energy coming to Earth without making contact in other ways first.

OUT OF CURIOSITY

A signal detected at a radio telescope in Ohio still puzzles SETI scientists over 45 years later. The so-called "Wow!" signal was a sudden burst of radio waves from the direction of Sagittarius, detected during a 1977 survey. It gets its name because astronomer Jerry R. Ehman wrote "Wow!" in the margin of the computer printout after he spotted it. Many attempts to find a natural explanation have failed, and searches for other signals from the region have been unsuccessful. Without more data, the "Wow!" signal remains unexplained.

MESSENGERS TO THE STARS

Another possible way to make contact with aliens is to send probes to other stars with information about Earth and its inhabitants. The few robot spacecraft that have already left the solar system carry messages of this kind in various formats, but these missions will take many thousands of years to fly close to another planetary system.

PIONEER PLAQUE

Probably the most famous message to the stars is the plaque carried onboard the Pioneer 10 and 11 probes. It includes pictures of a man and woman alongside the spacecraft, a scale of measurement, and maps to locate the solar system and Earth itself.

SIGNS OF CIVILIZATION

Astronomers are now looking for signs of life that do not rely on aliens sending signals on purpose. Aliens may give themselves away through huge engineering projects. For instance, an alien civilization might use technology to harvest energy from their sun using a structure called a **Dyson sphere** (right). This would affect a star's light output in ways that could be detected from Earth.

THE FATE OF THE UNIVERSE

What will happen to the Universe in the distant future? It depends on how the forces pulling the galaxy together and those forcing it apart are balanced. Trying to answer this question has led to one of the strangest discoveries in modern astronomy.

DISCOVERING DARK ENERGY

Until the late 1990s, most astronomers believed that the fate of the Universe depended on how much matter it contained. With a large enough amount of both visible and dark matter, gravity would slow down the expansion of the Universe and perhaps even reverse it. If there was too little matter, expansion would continue forever. In 1998, however, astronomers discovered a missing piece of the puzzle.

Astronomers measured the rate at which expansion is slowing down by detecting supernovae in distant galaxies. These exploding stars always release the same amount of energy, so their brightness seen from Earth indicates their distance and how long ago the explosion took place.

The distant explosions were fainter than expected, suggesting the supernovae were farther away. The only explanation was that cosmic expansion is speeding up due to an unknown effect that was named **dark energy**.

WHAT IS DARK ENERGY?

Astronomers have little idea of what dark energy is. One idea is that it's a fifth force of nature that pushes massive objects apart and gets stronger over larger distances. The other is that it's a built-in feature of space, a slight tendency to expand that only becomes noticeable over billions of light years.

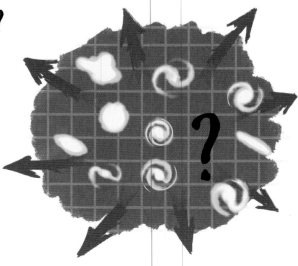

CRUNCH, CHILL, OR RIP?

The balance between gravity, cosmic expansion, and the accelerating effect of dark energy means that in the distant future, the Universe could meet its end in several possible ways. One thing it is unlikely to do is remain in the same state forever.

Big Crunch: If there's enough gravity to overcome expansion, the Universe could contract into a hot, dense ball, ending with an implosion from which another Universe might appear. The discovery of dark energy seems to rule this out because there's not enough matter in the Universe to overcome it.

Big Chill: If the Universe expands forever, then its distant future is dark and cold. After many generations of stars, the supply of hydrogen fuel to power new ones will run out, leaving a Universe of burned-out stars that will fade and disintegrate over trillions of years.

Big Rip: The latest measurements suggest that dark energy is growing stronger. If this continues, then billions of years into the future it might be felt on smaller scales, tearing apart galaxies, then planetary systems, then planets, and finally even atoms.

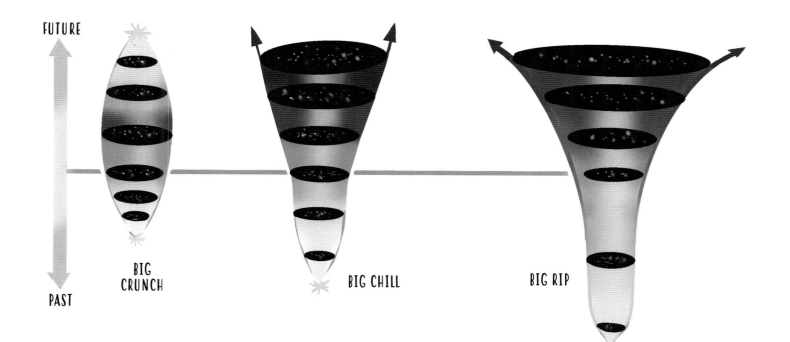

FUTURE

BIG CRUNCH

BIG CHILL

BIG RIP

PAST

Whatever the eventual fate of the Universe, it will continue for many billions of years. Space has been expanding throughout its history. Now, the edge of the observable Universe lies about 46 billion light years away. The Universe is so vast and so full of wonders and mysteries, there is more than enough to keep astronomers looking skyward.

GLOSSARY

absorption lines: Dark lines in a spectrum of light caused by atoms in the light's path absorbing certain colors and energies.

altazimuth: A way of measuring the angle above the horizon and east or west.

asteroid: A large chunk of space rock left over from the formation of the solar system.

astrolabe: An early device used by astronomers to measure angles in the sky.

axis: The line around which a planet turns.

Big Bang theory: Model for the origins of the Universe, in which everything was created in a superhot explosion 13.8 billion years ago.

black hole: A superdense space object formed by one or more collapsed stars, whose gravity is so strong that not even light can escape.

bolide: A bright, slow-moving meteor.

CNO cycle: A process that allows stars heavier than the Sun to generate energy at faster rates than smaller stars and shine more brightly.

comet: A chunk of mostly icy debris left over from the formation of the solar system.

corona: The superhot outer atmosphere of the Sun, whose gases are too faint to see except during a total solar eclipse.

dark energy: A mysterious effect causing the expansion of the Universe to speed up.

dark matter: A mysterious invisible substance known by the effect of its gravity.

declination: The angle of a sky object north or south of the celestial equator.

dwarf planet: A solar system object that has strong enough gravity to pull it into a sphere and share its orbit with other, smaller objects.

Dyson sphere: A structure built around a star in order to collect its energy.

eclipse: An event where a space object lines up with another and blocks its light.

ecliptic: An imaginary line around Earth's sky that the Sun seems to follow.

electromagnetic: A combination of electricity and magnetism.

emission lines: Bright lines revealed when light from space objects is spread into a spectrum.

epicycle: A circular path spinning around a center point fixed to another moving circle.

equatorial: System used to measure the positions of space objects in relation to the celestial equator.

event horizon: Edge of a black hole where gravity is so strong that light cannot escape.

exoplanet: Planet orbiting a star outside the solar system.

filament: Area of space where galaxy clusters and superclusters form a long chain or sheet.

Gamma ray: Electromagnetic wave similar to light, but which carries much more energy.

gravitational lensing: Effect that bends light rays passing close to heavy space objects.

gravitational waves: Distortions in the shape of space that can spread across the Universe.

inferior conjunction: When a planet crosses between the Sun and Earth.

infrared: Energy similar to light with slightly less energy.

lepton: Basic building block that makes up visible matter, such as a lightweight electron.

light year: Distance traveled by light in a year, about 9.5 trillion km or 5.9 trillion miles.

luminosity: Measure of the amount of light and other electromagnetic energy emitted by a star.

meridian: An imaginary line across the surface of a sphere linking its north and south poles.

meteor: Chunk of space dust or rock that burns up as it enters Earth's atmosphere.

meteorite: Space rock that lands on Earth.

nebula: Cloud of gas or dust in space.

neutron star: Superdense object with more than the mass of the Sun packed into a ball just a few km across.

nuclear fusion: A process in star cores, where lightweight atoms are forced together to make heavier elements and release energy.

Oort Cloud: Shell containing billions of comets outside the solar system.

parallax: Small shift in the direction of a star when seen from opposite sides of Earth's orbit.

phase: The amount of the Moon's Earth-facing side that is lit up by light from the Sun.

photosphere: Visible surface of a star.

planetary nebula: Glowing gas cloud created when a dying star blows away its outer layers.

pulsar: Fast-spinning neutron star that gives out light and other electromagnetic rays.

quark: One of the basic building blocks that make up all the matter in the Universe.

quasar: Galaxy that shines brightly as a giant black hole at its center pulls in stars and gas, and heats them to searing temperatures.

red giant: Enormous bright star with a relatively cool red surface.

redshift: Displacement of the spectrum of an astronomical object toward longer (red) wavelengths.

reflector: A telescope that collects light from distant objects using a curved mirror.

refractor: A telescope that collects light from distant objects using glass lenses.

right ascension: Angle of a sky object east or west of a fixed meridian line.

singularity: Object at center of a black hole with more mass than the Sun in a tiny space.

solar wind: Stream of particles blowing out from the surface of the Sun.

spectra: Rainbowlike band created by splitting a beam of light.

spectroscopic: Information about an object revealed by studying its spectrum.

supergiant: One of the biggest of all stars.

superior conjunction: When an inner planet lies on the opposite side of its orbit to Earth.

supernova: Explosion caused by a star core collapsing into a neutron star or a black hole.

ultraviolet: Type of energy similar to light but with more energy.

void: Huge, mostly empty region of the Universe.

white dwarf: Burned-out core of a star when it runs out of fuel and sheds its outer layers.

X-rays: Electromagnetic wave with more energy than ultraviolet but less than gamma.

zenith: Point in the sky directly above a stargazer's position on Earth.

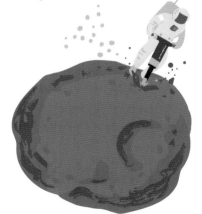

INDEX